# GameM
# Language:
## An In-Depth Guide

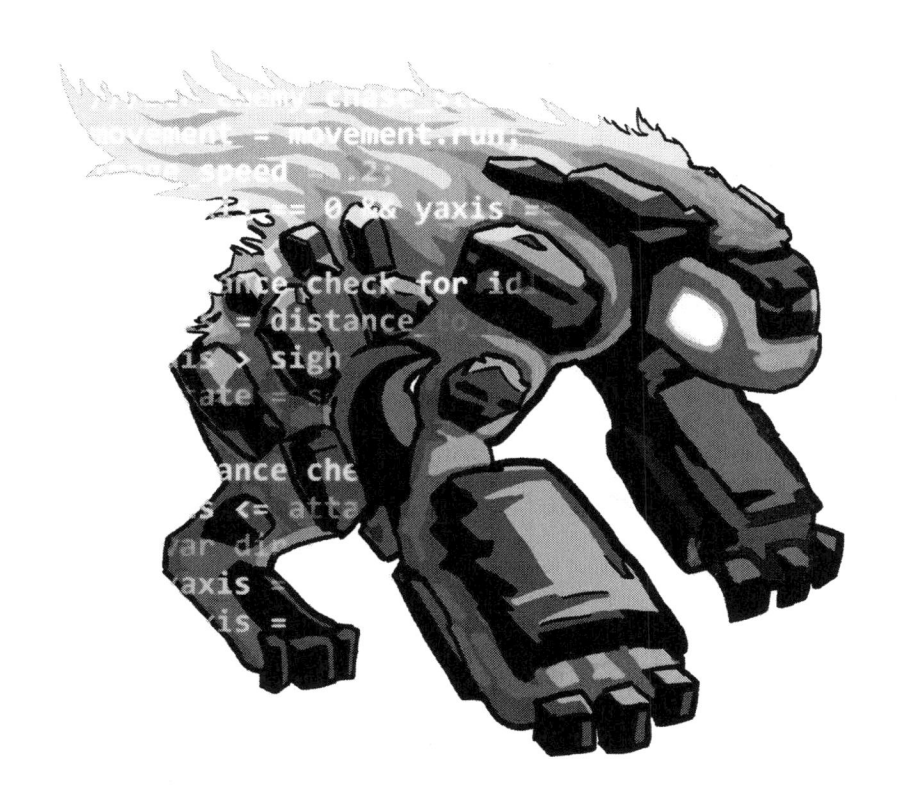

This book is dedicated to my beautiful wife, my beautiful daughter, and every aspiring game developer.

# Table of Contents

Preface: Introduction ............................................................. 6
Book: Contents ..................................................................... 17
Chapter 1: Lexical Structure ................................................ 21
Chapter 2: Data Types and Values ...................................... 29
Chapter 3: Variables ............................................................. 33
Chapter 4: Arrays and Data Structures .............................. 38
Chapter 5: Expressions and Operators ............................... 62
Chapter 6: Statements ......................................................... 70
Chapter 7: Scripts ................................................................. 79
Chapter 8: Objects and Sprites ........................................... 84
Chapter 9: Events ................................................................. 97
Chapter 10: Game Audio ................................................... 109
Chapter 11: Development Patterns and Tricks .............. 114
Chapter 12: Drawing on the GUI Layer ............................ 129
Chapter 13: Particles and Surfaces .................................. 137
Chapter 14: Physics ............................................................ 149
Chapter 15: Online Multiplayer ........................................ 160
Chapter 16: Artificial Intelligence .................................... 183
Contact and Kickstarter .................................................... 203

Preface
# Introduction

## The Author
Hey, guys! Good morning, afternoon, or evening, wherever and whenever you are! My name is Benjamin Anderson. You may know me from my YouTube channel, "HeartBeast," where I upload free GameMaker tutorial videos. Teaching GameMaker is my passion.

Let me tell you a little more about myself. I was raised in Vernal, Utah (where there are more cows than people). I grew up on a farm, but spent most of my days building small computer games in GameMaker. I finished my first recognized game, *Deep Magic*, at the age of 15 and published it for free on the YoYo Games sandbox website. There, it received nearly 18,000 downloads. Soon after finishing *Deep Magic*, I finished my second popular game, *Ancient War*, which was also published for free on the YoYo Games website and received over 27,000 downloads. You can find both of these games on GameJolt, but remember, I made them almost ten years ago, so don't expect anything too fancy.

During the next part of my life, I left for Rio de Janeiro, Brazil, where I lived for a couple of years to learn Portuguese, make new friends, and have an adventure. After returning from Brazil, I decided to pursue a career in computer science.

My favorite thing to do is program games and teach other people to do the same. I started a successful YouTube channel in January of 2014. I plan to continue learning more about GameMaker and sharing my knowledge with anyone who is willing to listen.

Outside of the computer world, I enjoy wakeboarding, playing chess, reading, writing, doing math, playing guitar, playing piano, singing, playing Pokémon, learning languages, and watching Psych or Castle with my wife.

## "Welcome, Game Designer."

There is something magical about game development that can't be found in any other creative medium. Everyone has their own reasons for enjoying this activity. For me, it's the god-like feeling I get when I create my own world and the satisfaction that comes from knowing my created world will follow the rules I've set. It's the sense of accomplishment I feel after spending hours on a frustrating problem and finally getting it to work and it's the joy that fills me when I see a smile on the face of someone exploring my creation. These are the reasons I spend most of my free time learning how to program and teaching what I've learned to anyone willing to learn.

Game creation in a digital form is a relatively unexplored medium. Whereas art and music have been around for as long as humans have, people of the current generation are the pioneers of this amazing new medium. It is easier to get started now than ever before. Our time is now.

## GameMaker Components

Welcome to square one. If you haven't ever used GameMaker before, this will be the most important section of this book. If you have used GameMaker, then you may want to skip this section, as much of it will be review. Below, I will briefly explain the basic resources that you will use while building a game.

# Sprites

A *sprite* in GameMaker refers to an image that represent an object in your game. Without sprites, all of the objects in the game would be invisible.

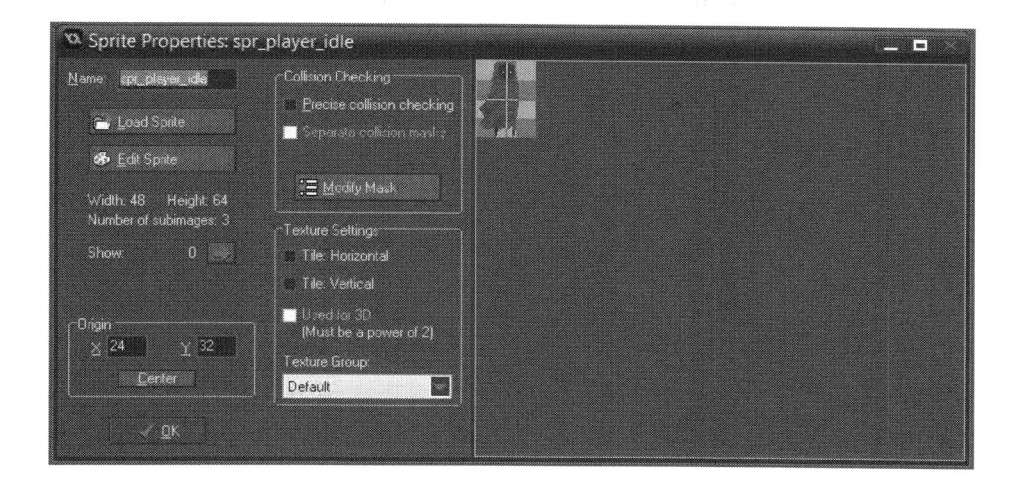

# Origin

Every sprite has an *origin*. The origin of a sprite is a reference point that determines the location at which the sprite is drawn, relative to the object it is assigned to. Quite often, the origin of a sprite will be set to "centered," resulting in a symmetrical flip if the sprite is mirrored.

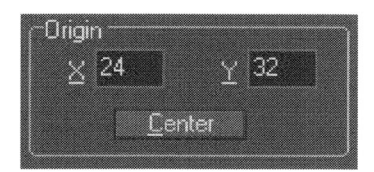

# Mask

A *mask* is used for collision detection by the object associated with the sprite. I most often use simple rectangular collision masks because they are the easiest to control and generally result in good-looking collisions. If you are a beginner, then *I suggest not clicking the "precise collision checking"* checkbox until you fully understand how it works; it can cause glitches in your game's collision checking and can also slow your game down because it is harder to compute.

8

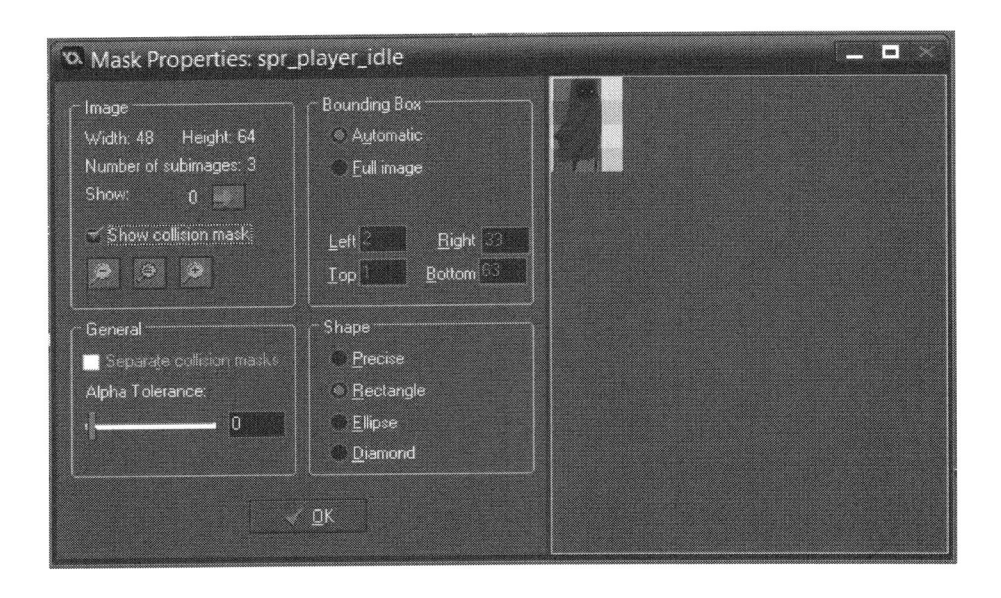

## Subimages

Sprites can be made up of multiple images, each of these images is called a *subimage*. When running a game, the sprite will cycle through these subimages to create an animation. The default speed of the sprite is set to 1 frame per step, but you can also adjust the speed of this animation. The speed is dependent on the speed of the game, that is, the room speed, which can also be changed.

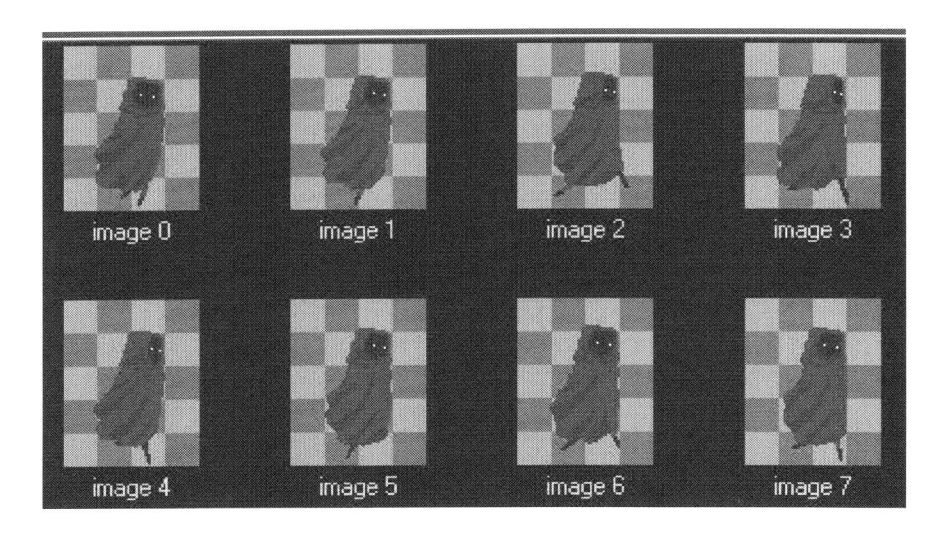

9

# Objects

*Objects* are central to the programming architecture of a GameMaker game. Objects in GameMaker interpret all of the events and run the majority of the code. Most objects have a sprite assigned to them. When you place an object in your level, the thing you will see displayed in the game will be the (first subimage of the) sprite associated with that object.

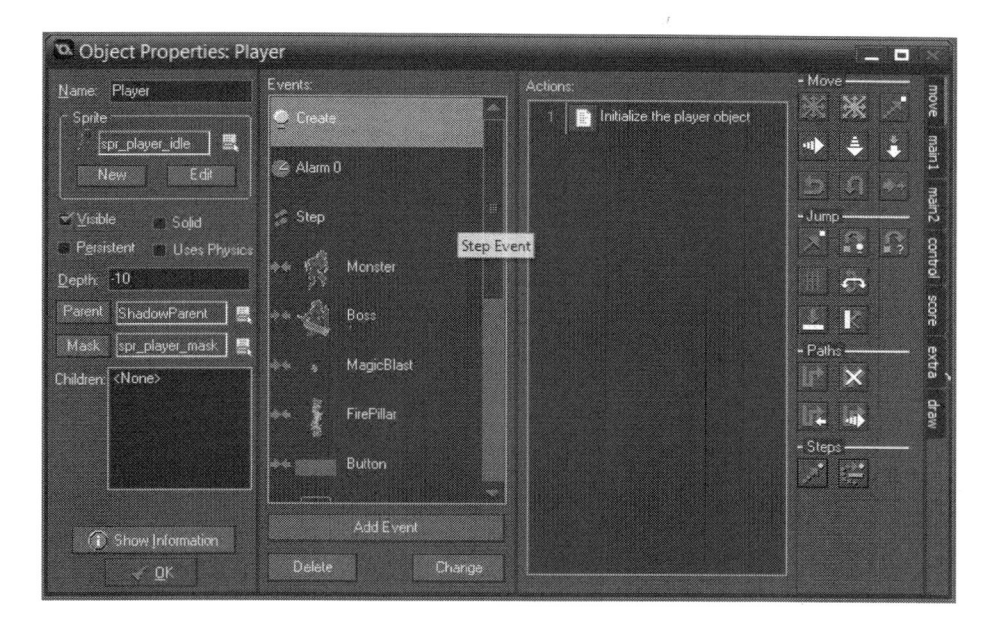

## Events

*Events* control the behavior of each object. An event is a condition that is met during the game; each event can trigger an action (more on actions below). An example of an event would be the **Game Start Event**. This event is triggered at the very moment the game starts running. It can run code in an action that is relevant to the start of the game, such as showing a start screen.

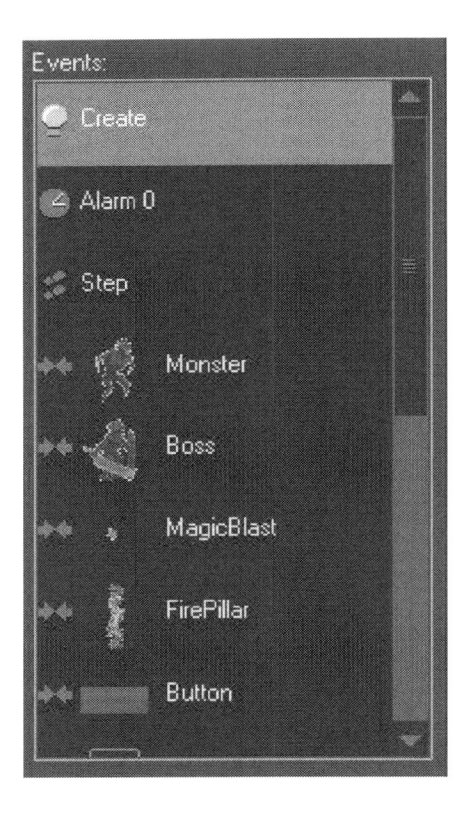

## Actions

*Actions* are what happen when an event occurs. GameMaker has a large variety of drag-and-drop actions that can be used. In this book, I will not be talking about drag-and-drop actions very much; there are already some excellent books available that teach you how to use them. There is one drag-and-drop action that you will be using quite often: the **Execute Code Action**. This is the action that runs GameMaker's scripting language, GML (short for GameMaker Language). All of the code examples in this book will either be run in an **Execute Code Action** or inside a script (more on

11

scripts later). The **Execute Code Action** is located in the "Control" tab under "Code" in an object's properties.

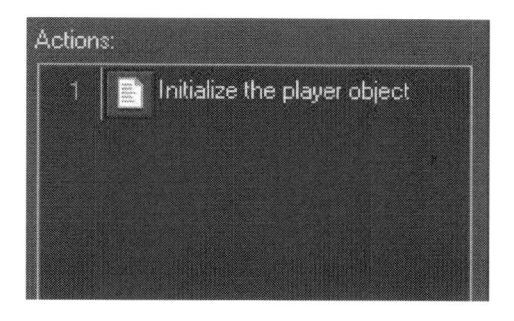

## Timelines

A *timeline* is a list of moments (points in time) in a game. At each moment, you can set an action to be executed. Timelines are useful for controlling sequences of actions. I like to use them for artificial intelligence sequences. For example, you have an enemy that runs up to you, jumps forward to attack, and jumps back. This short sequence could be defined using a timeline.

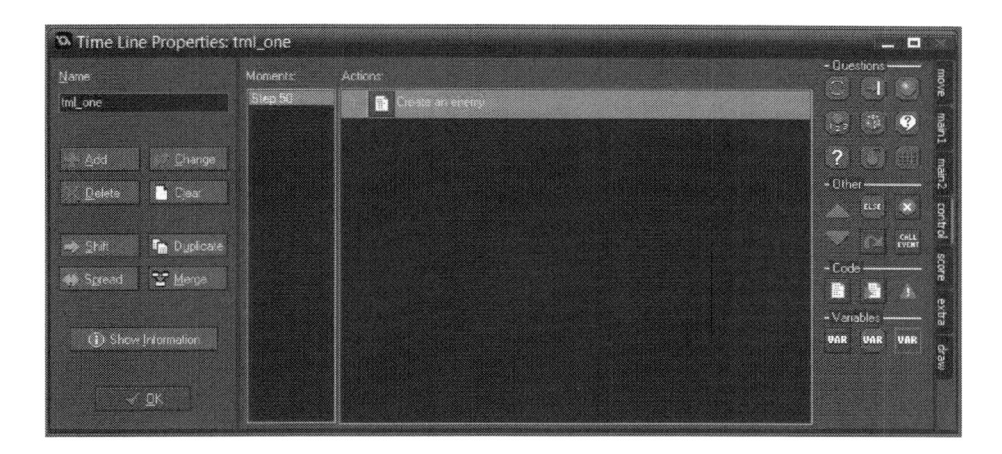

## Fonts

You can use this resource to create different *fonts* for your game, changing the way that text appears. You can set the size and style for your fonts. Fonts can be accessed in your game using the font resource's name.

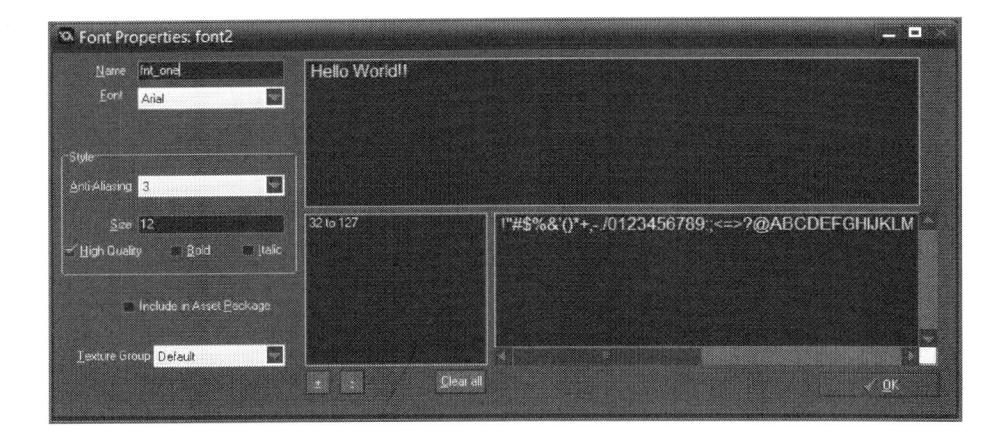

## Sounds

*Sounds*, just like sprites, can add very important feedback to your game. Sounds can be played on a loop or played only a single time. Adding high quality sounds will make just as much of a difference to the feel of your game as adding high quality sprites.

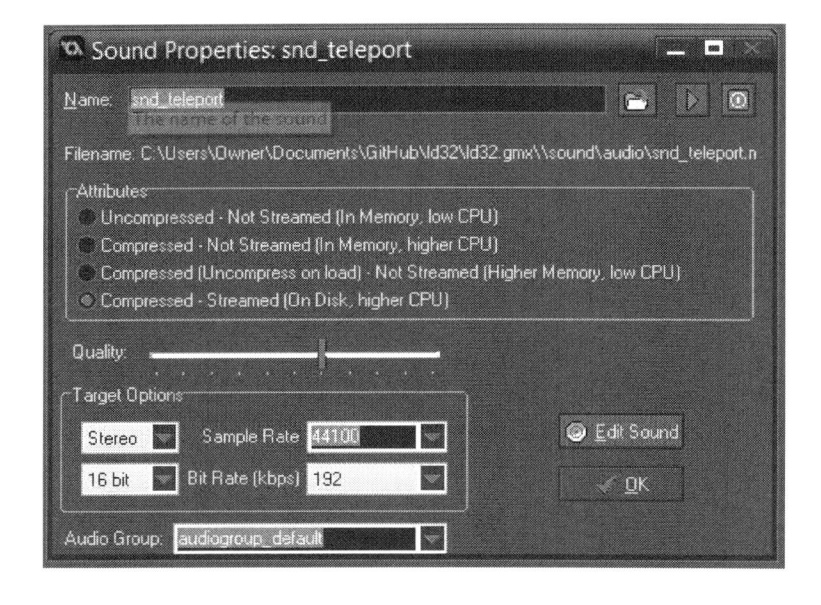

13

# Rooms

*Rooms* contain the levels of your game. Each room can be filled with objects at different locations. You can also use rooms to create menus, stat screens, and inventory screens. Rooms have a height and width and can also employ backgrounds and views (more on these below).

# Backgrounds

*Backgrounds* are similar to sprites; however, a background is associated with a room in the game, not any specific object. You can add a background to a room in the room properties.

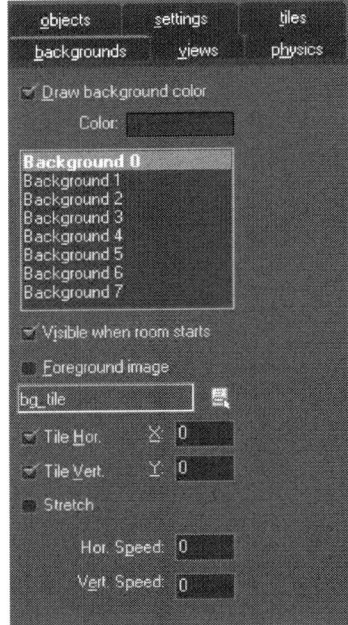

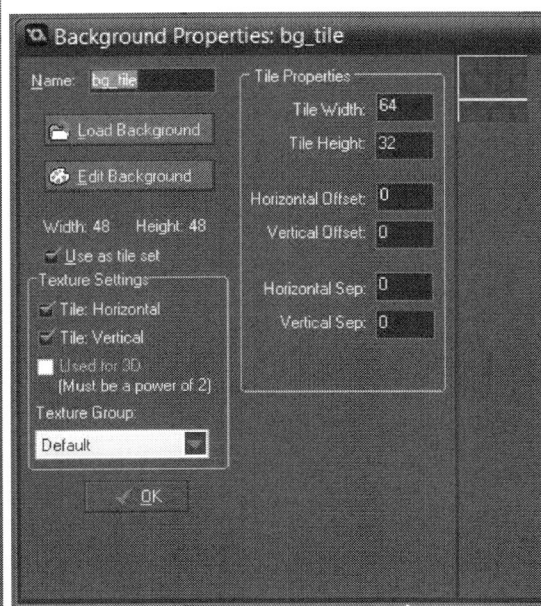

# Views

A *view* is a section of a room that can be displayed on the screen. There are many times in games when you don't want the player to see the entire level; you can create a view inside the room that restricts what the player can see. Views have a height and width that set how much of the room is visible. Views also have a port height and port width that define the size of the game window on your screen.

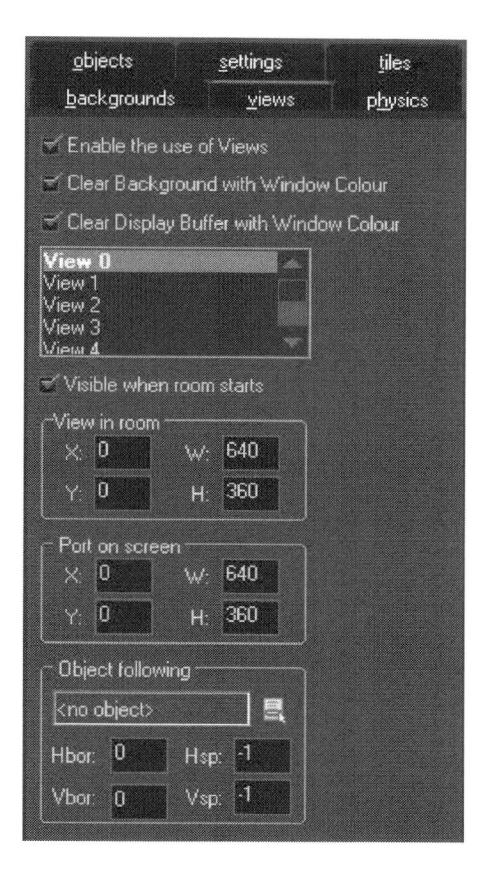

# Book
# Contents

## What is in this book?
This book as a mixture of prose, simple code examples, images, and actual game examples. At the start of the book, I use mainly images, prose, and simple code examples to get you started on learning how GameMaker Language works. Later, I start to give more complicated examples that involve building mini-games or basic game engines.

## Chapter 1: Lexical Structure
In Chapter 1, you will learn to understand comments, literals, identifiers, and some of the rules that must be followed while writing code in GameMaker Language.

## Chapter 2: Data Types
Chapter 2 covers the different data types and values that you can use in GameMaker Language. This information will become more important as you learn both the different functions available in GameMaker and the types of data you should pass into each function.

## Chapter 3: Variables and Scope
Chapter 3 will give you a solid understanding of variables, including type and scope. You will learn that GameMaker is a weakly typed language and how that influences the way you program.

## Chapter 4: Data Structures and Arrays
In Chapter 4, your brain will probably explode as you attempt to absorb all the information about data structures and arrays. Chapter 4 is a tricky chapter, but it is also very rewarding because it will prepare you for networking in GameMaker Language.

## Chapter 5: Expressions and Operators
Chapter 5 will teach you the different expressions and operators that you have at your disposal when writing in GML. Many of these operators are common to other programming languages, and a solid understanding of how they work is essential to writing powerful code in GameMaker Language.

## Chapter 6: Statements
When you reach Chapter 6, you will be ready to use all that you have learned up to that point to create different statements in GameMaker Language. These statements will help you define the logic of your game. Statements, like operators, are necessary for any large GameMaker project.

## Chapter 7: Scripts
In Chapter 7, you will quickly learn of the power of GameMaker scripts. Scripts execute blocks of code and are used to cut out redundancies that may make your code bloated and hard to maintain. Writing the same type of code in all of your separate objects can become difficult to maintain and waste your time. Scripts will give you the power to write code in one place and then call that code in multiple locations (as needed).

## Chapter 8: Objects and Sprites
As you read through Chapter 8, you will learn all about objects in GameMaker and their relationships with sprites. Objects and sprites are two of the main building blocks of any game; both have many different built-in variables and properties that you will want to become familiar with.

## Chapter 9: Events
Chapter 9 will cover the basics of GameMaker events. You will learn how events control the execution of code and which events are used most often. You will also learn how to create and run customized events.

## Chapter 10: Game Audio
Chapter 10 gets you started with playing sounds in your game. I'll teach you the basic functions you need for audio and a few other functions you will use to create audio emitters that can modify your sounds while your game is running.

## Chapter 11: Patterns, Tricks, and Tips
Chapter 10 is full of basic patterns, functions, tips, and tricks, including tricks for getting input from the player, how to control zoomed views, how to make an object follow the mouse, and how to make an object point towards the mouse (among many others).

## Chapter 12: Surfaces and Particles
In Chapter 12, you will learn how to create amazing graphic effects in your game using the power of surfaces and particles. I'll show you how to create and manipulate surfaces. In the section on particles, I'll teach you how to create your own particle systems, particle types, and emitters (and we'll figure out what these terms even mean).

## Chapter 13: HUD and GUI
In this chapter, you will learn how to draw information such as health, lives, and score on the screen. You will learn more specifically about the `Draw GUI Event` inside GameMaker and how it works differently from all other draw events.

## Chapter 14: Physics
This chapter is all about GameMaker's built-in physics engine and how you can use it to start building some very realistic games. I'll show you how to build a simple boxes-under-gravity example and then move on to a more complicated truck-and-randomly-generated-terrain example. This chapter was loads of fun to write and I'm sure you will enjoy reading it.

## Chapter 15: Online Multiplayer
In this chapter, I start by explaining some common terms that you will need to understand in order to build your first online multiplayer game. Next, I'll walk you through a couple of examples. The first example is simple and can't really be classified as a complete game, but it is great for learning the

basics of network communication. After that, I'll show you how to build a simple, turn-based board game.

## Chapter 16: Artificial Intelligence
This chapter is dedicated to all the different types of artificial intelligence. I'll cover basic top-down artificial intelligence, some options for platform artificial intelligence, some basic pathfinding, and a few other considerations when you are programming those baddies.

# Chapter 1
# Lexical Structure

You might think that "lexical" is a big word. Well, I guess it isn't really that big, but it definitely doesn't come up often in everyday conversation. *Lexical* refers to the vocabulary of a language. In this chapter, I will teach you the basic vocabulary of GameMaker Language.

## Comments

A *comment* in GameMaker Language is a section of text that is completely ignored by the *compiler* (the part of GameMaker that turns your code into a game); in other words, comments don't do anything for your game. Comments are useful to programmers because there are times when it is beneficial to describe a piece of code.

### Adding Comments to Code

There are three ways to declare a comment in GameMaker Language. The first is to place two forward slashes, //, before the line of code. This will *comment out* (we say "comment out" to remind ourselves that the **comment** is *out* of the consideration of the compiler) any characters on the line after the two slashes.

```
// This is a comment on its own line
var i=0; // This is a comment after some code
```

The second way to comment allows you to comment out multiple lines of the code. This kind of comment starts with a forward slash that is followed by an asterisk, /*, and finishes with an asterisk that is followed by a forward slash, */.

21

```
/* Here is a comment
that spans a
few lines */
```

The third way to add a comment is similar to the first, but it has some functionality that is specific to GameMaker Language. This type of comment is declared by placing three forward slashes, ///, before the line of code. It works similar to the first type, but **when this comment is placed on the the first line of a code, it has additional benefits**.

```
/// This is a comment with added benefits.
```

The added benefits you get depend on whether the comment is on the first line of an **Execute Code Action** or on the first line of a script.

If the comment is on the first line of an **Execute Code Action**, it will be shown as the description text of that action. You can use this kind of comment to label code actions and make it easier to navigate and maintain your code. Let me give you a screenshot example. I have this comment on the first line of my code.

```
/// Initialize all the data
```

This is what the description of the **Code Action** looks like because of that comment:

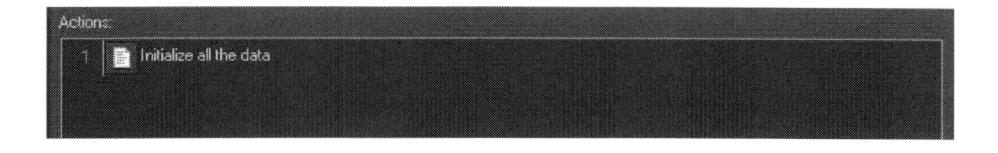

Actions:
1. Initialize all the data

If the comment is on the first line of a script, the comment will be shown as *helper text* (a pop-up that tells you which elements are needed) when calling the script elsewhere in your game. Here is an example of what the comment might look like inside the script itself:

```
/// scr_add(number1,number2)
```

Here is what you will see while calling the script in GameMaker because of the comment at the top of the script; you get descriptive code completion for the script, like this:

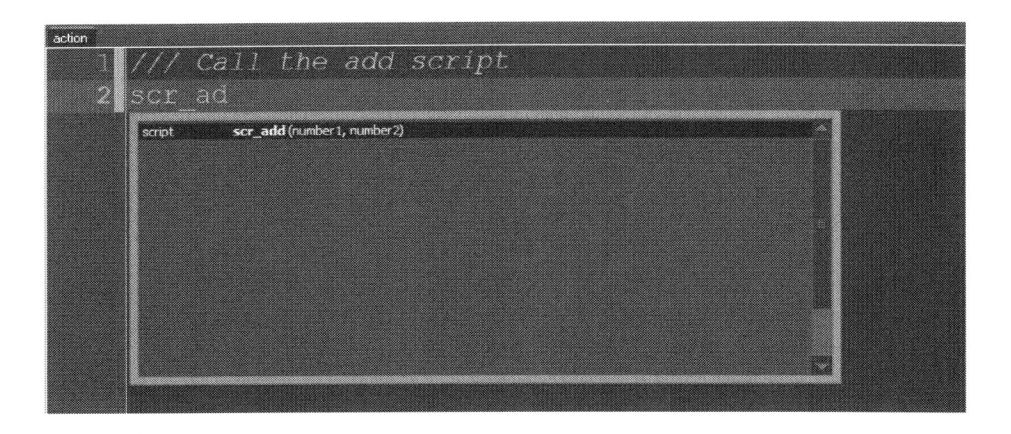

```
/// Call the add script
scr_ad
    script    scr_add (number1, number2)
```

And, on top of that, you get argument helper text down at the bottom of the code editor while you are typing in the arguments (just like for all other GameMaker functions).

If that doesn't make sense, you are probably just new to scripts. That's okay! Just come back and reread this section after you have finished the chapter on scripts (Chapter 7).

23

## Best Practices for Comments

In the world of commenting code, there are two extremes. On the one extreme, there are programmers who comment every line of code to describe exactly what that line of code does. For example:

```
// Set health to 100
health=100;
```

Because the code is already pretty clear, these types of comments are, at best, redundant and, at worst, a waste of effort. On the other extreme, there are programmers who never use comments. This is very common among new programmers because at the time of writing their code, it all makes perfect sense. The problem is, later on, uncommented code is more difficult to maintain.

The best advice I that can give is to write your comments as if there were another programmer looking through your code (and maybe there will be). Keep the code clean, but try to explain the *why* behind the more complicated sections and not just the *how*.

Hopefully, these few pages have convinced you of the benefits of using comments, while also persuading you to take advantage of those benefits.

## Literals

A *literal* is a value that appears directly in your code. Here are some examples of what literals look like inside GameMaker Language:

```
true              // The boolean value true
false             // The boolean value false
3                 // A real number
3.5               // Another real number
"GameMaker!"      // A double-quote string
'Language'        // A single-quote string
```

## Identifiers

*Identifiers* are names given to variables. Here is an example of how to use an identifier:

```
age=25;
```

Do you recognize what part of this code is the identifier? It's the word "age". The number **25** represents the *literal value* of the variable and the word "age" is the *name* or *identifier*. Identifiers are a fairly simple concept and, for the most part, you can choose whatever descriptive word you want for the identifier. However, there are some restrictions. I also have a few words of advice for choosing identifiers.

## Identifier Restrictions

There are five main restrictions on what you can use as an identifier. Don't worry about memorizing them. As you start creating more and more variables, you will start to get a feel for what options you have. Here is the list:

1. Identifiers cannot exceed 64 characters
2. Identifiers cannot contain special characters
3. Identifiers cannot contain spaces
4. Identifiers cannot begin with a number (They can contain them, though.)
5. Identifiers cannot share the same name as another resource in GameMaker (e.g., `obj_player`)

## Identifier Tips

GameMaker Studio uses a naming practice called *snake case* for most of its built-in variables and functions. The pattern for naming a variable in snake case has easy rules. Here they are:

1. Every letter be lowercase
2. Replace every space be replaced with an underscore

Here is an example of an identifier in snake case:

```
my_name="Ben";
```

Simple, right? I often use snake case when naming my variables and resources because I want to be consistent with the patterns used in the native GameMaker variables and functions. This does not mean that this is the only way to name things. In fact, many people only use other naming conventions so that they can more easily separate their variables and functions from the built-in ones.

Another common naming convention is called *camel case*. There are only three rules for camel case and they might already be familiar to you.

1. Remove all spaces
2. Make sure the first word begins with a lowercase letter
3. Make sure all other words begin with an uppercase letter

Here is an example:

```
myName="Ben";
```

Regardless of what style you choose, the **most important** thing is that you are **consistent**! I'm serious. If you are not consistent, you will get messed up later when you are trying to remember what you named certain variables.

## Case Sensitivity

GameMaker Language is a case-sensitive language. Two identifiers with different cases are different identifiers. You may have a variable called **hp** and a different variable called **HP**.

```
hp=100;
HP=200;
```

26

These two variables are **different**. If you try to use the identifier HP to access hp, you will either get the wrong value (if HP has been defined) or get an error (if HP has not been defined).

## Reserved Words

In GameMaker, there are some words that can't be used as identifiers because they are reserved for built-in variables. Some of the common reserved words are:

```
gravity
x
y
health
exp
direction
speed
```

The variables affect the player object in a way that you may not want in certain cases. Because of this, many programmers use modified versions to get around the reserved words.

```
grav
player_x
player_y
hp
expr
dir
spd
```

## Optional Semicolons

In GameMaker Language, placing a semicolon at the end of your statement is optional. In most programming languages, however, this is not the case. In GameMaker Language, these two statements are equivalent:

```
x=0; // A statement with a semicolon
x=0  // A statement without a semicolon
```

I would *highly* recommend getting into the habit of placing semicolons after every statement because many other major programming languages require it.

# Chapter 2
# Data Types and Values

## Number Literals
A *number literal* is a number inside your code. Here are some examples of number literals:

```
35
3.75555
-3
```

## Working with Numbers
Working with numbers in GameMaker Language is similar to working with numbers on a calculator. You can perform all of the standard operations such as addition, subtraction, multiplication, and division. There are also some other operations and functions that you can perform on numbers. Here are a few examples of some common operations and functions:

```
18+7      // Adds 7 to 18
30-5      // Subtracts 5 from 30
5*5       // Multiplies 5 by 5
100/4     // Divides 100 by 4
20%3      // Returns the remainder of 20 divided by 3, which is 2

round(5.6);   // Rounds 5.6 up to 6
round(5.3);   // Rounds 5.3 down to 5
floor(5.6);   // Rounds 5.6 down to 5
ceil(5.3);    // Rounds 5.3 up to 6
abs(-4);      // Returns the absolute value of -4

sign(-4);     // Returns a -1 for a negative number and a
              // +1 for a positive number
```

```
random(10);          // Returns a random number between 0 and 10
irandom(10);         // Returns a random integer from 0 to 10
random_range(5,10);  // Returns a random number from 5 to 10
irandom_range(5,10); // Returns a random integer from 5 to 10
```

## String Literals

A *string literal* is a list of zero or more characters surrounded by single or double quotation marks. Here are some examples of string literals:

```
"Ben"
"3"
'GameMaker'
' '
```

Note that the string literal **"3"** is different from the number literal **3**. Later in this chapter, I will talk about the importance of knowing the difference between (and how to convert between) the two literal types.

## Working with Strings

Knowing how to work with strings can be useful, but it can also be a little confusing at first. Unlike number values, strings behave differently than might be expected. Let's look at some examples.

```
'Benjamin'+'Anderson'; // gives 'BenjaminAnderson'
'4' + '8';             // gives '48', NOT 12 or '12'
```

## Converting between Reals and Strings

In GameMaker Language, it is critical to understand conversion between reals (numbers) and strings because it won't happen automatically. This is a very common issue for new developers. Let's look at how you can convert between the two so that you never have a problem with it.

```
string(3); // Converts number 3 into the string '3'
real('3'); // Converts the string '3' it into the number 3
```

Why would it be important to use these functions? One of the most common reasons is to draw number values, such as the player's stats, on the screen.

```
hp = 100;
// This is incorrect and will give an error
draw_text(x,y-32, 'HP: ' + hp);
```

If you were to put this code in your game, it would give an error. The **draw_text** function needs a string value to be able to draw to the screen, but our variable **hp** currently holds a number value. To get this to work, you will need to convert the number to a string like this:

```
hp=100;
// This is correct
draw_text(x,y-32, 'HP: ' + string(hp));
```

## Boolean Values

A *boolean value* has only two states: booleans are either true or false; they can't be anything else. Here is an example of a boolean:

```
in_air=false;
moving=true;
```

Simple, right? The name can often be intimidating, but there really isn't much to them. Here is an in-game example of how you might use the **in_air** boolean:

31

```
if (in_air==true) {
    sprite_index=spr_player_jumping;
}
```

This code checks the boolean variable **in_air** to find out if the player is jumping. If the player is jumping, it changes the object's sprite to a jumping sprite.

There aren't very many basic data types in GameMaker because the language is weakly typed, and so, there are implicit type conversions happening (almost magically) behind the scenes, where you don't have to worry about them. This is nice, but a good understanding of the few basic types that GameMaker uses will help improve your ability to program error free in GameMaker Language.

# Chapter 3
# Variables

## Variables

*Variables* in GameMaker Language (and in other programming languages) are used to store information in memory. Once a piece of information (or value) is stored, it can later be accessed and manipulated; this helps create code that is easier to understand and maintain. Skilled use of variables creates powerful code.

## Variable Typing

Variable typing shows up in many programming languages. Generally, when you create a new variable, the compiler will want to know if that variable is going to be used to hold a string value, a number value, a boolean value, or any other type of value available in the language. This can be confusing for new programmers, so variables in GameMaker Language were designed to be weakly typed. This means that you don't need to declare the type of a variable when you create it. It also means that a variable that was once used to hold a number value can (at any time in your code) be told to hold a string value.

Even this basic understanding of variable typing will help you to avoid errors as you use GameMaker Language.

## Variable Declaration

Declaring a variable in GameMaker is easy. There are a few different ways to declare them and I will talk about these different ways in the next section. For the most part, all you have to do is name the variable with an identifier; use the assignment operator, a single equals sign, =; and then include a value. Here is an example of some of the ways that you can define a variable.

```
name="Benjamin"; // String variable type
age=25; // Number variable type
happy=true; // Boolean variable type
```

The next section will talk more about variable declaration and describe how to declare variables in different scopes.

## Variable Scope

The *scope* of a variable describes the locations in the code where you have access to that variable. In GameMaker Language, there are three main variable scopes. There is the *global scope*, the *instance scope*, and the *local scope*.

## Global Variables

If a variable is created in the global scope, it can be accessed from anywhere in the code. Variables within the global scope are called *global variables* (**big** surprise there). These variables are defined by placing the keyword **global** and a dot, **.**, before the variable identifier.

```
global.name="Benjamin Anderson";
```

After the global variable has been created, you can access it from within any script or object.

## Instance Variables

If a variable is created in the instance scope, it can only be accessed within the code of a single instance. Variables located in the instance scope are called *instance variables*. It is best to define these variables in the **Create Event** of the object in order to avoid errors caused by undefined variables. There is no secret to defining these variables; you simply name the variable with an identifier and then assign a value to it.

```
name="Benjamin Anderson";
```

After declaring them in an object, you can access instance variables elsewhere inside the object.

In older versions of GameMaker, instance variables had to be defined in the **Create Event** of an object or the compiler would throw an error.

## Local Variables

If a variable is created in the local scope, it can only be accessed within the action or script in which it was defined. Variables located in the local scope are called local variables. Defining a local variable is just like defining an instance variable, only you place the **var** keyword before the identifier.

```
var name="Benjamin Anderson";
```

Local variables didn't exist in older versions of GameMaker. If you try to create a local variable in an older version, you will get an error.

## Macros (Formerly Constants)

A macro is similar to a variable because it can contain a value that is accessible in the code. A macro is different from a variable because it can only have one value: once you set the value of a macro, it cannot be modified during the game. In many programming languages, the identifier for the macro is written in all caps. This helps the programmer to distinguish it from other variables, primarily as a reminder that it cannot be altered.

To define a macro, you will need to click on the macro's node in the resource tree. There are two nodes that you can choose from. I use the macro node labeled "Default" Once the macro window comes up, you can use the add button to create as many or few as you will need. After the macro has been defined, you can use it inside your code just like any other variable.

35

```
draw_text(x,y,COMPANY_NAME );
```

It should also be noted that **macros fall under the global scope** and can be used anywhere in the code.

# Enums

*Enums* are a rather new (and very useful) part of GameMaker Language. The word enum is short for enumerator; an enum enumerates (or lists) a set of key-value pairs. Let's look at how you can create one.

```
enum basestat {
        hp=50,
        att=20,
        def=18,
        spd=24
}
```

Easy enough. After you have created the enum, you can access the values in it like this.

```
var basehp=basestat.hp; // Returns 50
```

It's important to know that **enums, like macros, are global in scope, so they can be accessed anywhere in your code**. They are constants, meaning that they cannot hold values that will change. Enums also have default values, so you don't have to assign a value to them. You could create an enum with default values like this:

```
enum months {
        January,
        February,
        March,
        April,
```

```
        May,
        June,
        July,
        August,
        September,
        October,
        November,
        December
}
```

The default values start at **1** and count up. In this example, **month.January** now has a value of **1** and **month.December** has a value of **12**.

In a later chapter, I will show you some ways to use enums in combination with arrays to give your code better structure and also make it easier to read.

## Undefined Variables

An undefined variable is one that has never had a value assigned to it. These types of variables will show up quite often when you are first learning to program because you will try to call a variable that has not yet been defined and the compiler will throw an error. If you read the error message carefully, it will tell you the object (and often, the exact line of code) where the error occurred.

# Chapter 4
# Arrays and Data Structures

## Arrays

An *array* is a kind of variable that can hold more than one value. Easy, right? Let me see if I can give you an idea of what I'm talking about. Here is an example of some ordinary (that is, single-valued) variables and then an example of an array:

```
// Ordinary variables
var name1='Ben';
var name2='Charly';
var name3='Dalin';

// Array
var names;
names[0]='Ben';
names[1]='Charly';
names[2]='Dalin';
```

If you imagine that the array **names** refers to a row of small boxes in which each box has its own label (an index) and its own content (some data), then you are imagining what an array might look like in physical form. Here is an image that can help you to visualize it:

```
                    Indexes
                       ↓
        0              1              2
    ┌───────┐      ┌───────┐      ┌───────┐
    │       │      │       │      │       │
    │ 'Ben' │      │'Charly'│     │'Dalin'│
    │       │      │       │      │       │
    └───────┘      └───────┘      └───────┘
                       ↑
                     Data
```

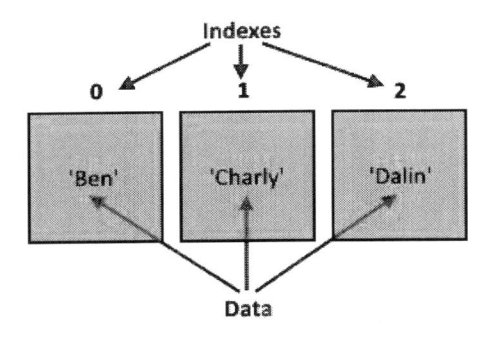

If you have never used an array before, then, at this point, you are probably wondering how an array is better than multiple variables. The main reason that arrays are better is that you can loop through them. I will talk about loops more later, but for now, let me explain just the basics.

What if you wanted to display these names on the screen? Here is how you would do it with the list of ordinary variables:

```
draw_text(32,32,name1);
draw_text(32,64,name2);
draw_text(32,96,name3);
```

Not too complicated right? In this case, it isn't a problem because there are only three names, but what if there were 100 names? The coding would become pretty tedious. Now, let's look at how you can display the names with an array and a loop.

```
var i=0;
repeat(3) {
        draw_text(32,32*(i+1),names[i]);
        i++;
}
```

I won't go into great detail explaining the loop, but know that this code does exactly what the code above does, only it uses an array. The benefit of this code is that, if there are 100 names, all you have to do is change

39

the number in **repeat()**, like so:

```
var i=0;
repeat(100) {
        draw_text(32,32*(i+1),names[i]);
        i++;
}
```

Super cool, huh? This code is way better than typing 100 statements with only slight differences.

Arrays are extremely powerful. The value within the square brackets, [ ], of the array contains what is called the array's *index*. This number indicates what location in the array to read data from (or write data to). The index of the array starts at 0 and counts up from there. *It is important to remember that the first index of an array will be at position "0", not position "1".*

## Array-Related Functions

In GameMaker Language, there are a few different functions that let you manipulate arrays. There aren't very many, so I will cover them all here. The first function, **is_array**, allows you to check to see if a variable is actually an array.

```
var a;
a[0]=0;
a[1]=0;

if (is_array(a)) {
        show_message('The variable is an array');
} else {
        show_message('The variable is NOT an array');
}
```

This function returns a boolean (true-or-false) value indicating whether or not the variable passed to it is an array.

The other function (one that I, personally, use more often) is
`array_length_1d`.

```
var a;
a[0]=0;
a[1]=0;

show_message('The size of the array is:
'+string(array_length_1d(a));
```

This function returns the array's size (as a number). You may wonder why the function has **_1d** at the end of it. The reason is that GameMaker supports both one-dimensional (1d) arrays and two-dimensional (2d) arrays. So far, you have only seen 1d arrays; however, 2d arrays are at least as powerful as 1d arrays (and can sometimes be even more powerful). Let's move on and learn a little about 2d arrays.

## Two-Dimensional Arrays

A 2d array is an array with two indexes. If a 1d array can be thought of as a row of data, with each index representing a position in the row, a 2d array is like a grid of data, where each index-index pair represents a location in the grid.

## Different Data Structures in GameMaker

GameMaker Studio has some amazing data structures available; here is a list of them:

```
stacks
queues
lists
maps
priority queues
grids
```

Each of these data structures is a unique tool, and each can be applied to different data storage scenarios. I have used many of them in my own game projects. This section of the chapter is necessary to understand the chapter on multiplayer games. Make sure to pay close attention if you are interested in making multiplayer games.

## Stacks

*Stacks* are data structures that can be found in many programming languages. A stack is a last-in-first-out (LIFO) data structure. If you remove one slice of data from the stack, it will be the most-recently-added slice of data that gets removed. Imagine a deck of cards where you can only add or remove cards from the top. Here is an image that might help you to imagine how a stack works:

### Last In, First Out (LIFO)

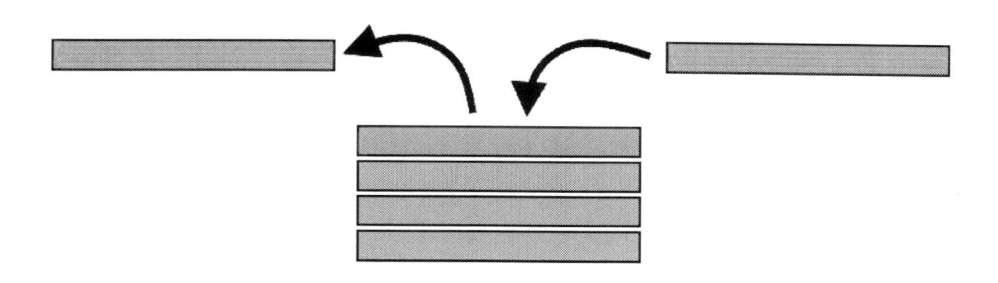

The code below shows you how to create a stack in GameMaker Language. This line of code will create a stack and then assign its id to the **my_stack** variable so that you can access it later through that variable.

```
my_stack=ds_stack_create();
```

It is important to destroy data structures when you are done using them, because they can take up a lot of memory, even to the point of crashing your game. Here is how you can destroy the stack when you are finished with it:

```
ds_stack_destroy(my_stack);
```

There are the two methods used to add or remove data from a stack. When working with stacks, adding data is referred to as "pushing" and removing data is referred to as "popping." Using our card analogy, pushing is like adding a card to the top of the deck, and popping is like removing a card from the top of the deck. Here is the function you use to push a value to the stack:

```
ds_stack_push(my_stack,3);
```

I recommend making sure that the stack has data before attempting to call a pop method. Here is how you pop the top piece of data from the stack (if and only if it is not empty):

```
if (!ds_stack_empty(my_stack)) {
       var number=ds_stack_pop(my_stack);
}
```

Sometimes, you may want to check the value on the top of the stack before you pop it (calling the pop function will remove the data from the data structure, but this function will leave the data alone, a little like just peeking at the top card of the deck).

```
var number=ds_stack_top(my_stack);
```

To clear the stack of all of its values, simply call this function:

```
ds_stack_clear(my_stack);
```

You can copy stacks as well.

```
my_newstack=ds_stack_create();
ds_stack_copy(my_newstack, my_stack);
```

Lastly, you can find out how many data elements (cards) there are in the stack.

```
var stack_size=ds_stack_size(my_stack);
```

## Using a Stack for a Card Game

Now that you've seen the basic functions used for manipulating a stack, I'm going to show you how we can use a stack to build a card game. I have simplified this example as much as I can so that we can focus on the stack data structure.

We will need to create a few sprites for this example. They can be as simple as different colored squares. I made my sprites rectangular to make them look like cards, but you can create them however you like.

- `spr_card_red`
- `spr_card_green`
- `spr_card_blue`
- `spr_deck`

I made my deck an off-white color, representing the back of a card. We can keep these really simple, but using different colors will help us visualize how stacks work in a game.

Now that we have the sprites, it is time to create the objects. We will need three objects. Here is what I chose to name them:

- `obj_deck`
- `obj_card`
- `obj_drag_controller`

Once we have created these three objects, we are ready to start programming. Open the deck object, add a **Create Event** to it, and drag

44

over an `Execute Code Action` from the control tab on the right (this is where we will create our stack).

**obj_deck: Create Event**

```
/// Create the stack data structure
deck=ds_stack_create();
```

This line of code creates a new stack and assigns it to the variable **deck**.

Now, we are going to leave the deck object for a bit and open up the drag controller object. Once we have the drag controller object open, we can add a new `Create Event` to it and drag over an `Execute Code Action`. In this action, we are going to create a variable for controlling our drag-and-drop card movement.

**obj_drag_controller: Create Event**

```
/// Create a global variable to keep track
// of the card we are drawing
global.card=noone;
```

This global variable will hold the value of the card instance that we are dragging with the mouse. Once we have a reference to the instance, we can make it follow the mouse in a `Step Event`.

**obj_drag_controller: End Step Event**

```
/// Move the card
if (global.card!=noone) {
        with (global.card) {
                x=mouse_x;
                y=mouse_y;
        }
}
```

This code performs an important check before trying to access the **global.card** instance. It first checks to make sure that we actually have a card. If we do, then it sets the x and y positions of that card equal to the x

45

and y positions of the mouse. This code is placed in the **End Step Event** for draw timing reasons. If we place it in the **Step Event**, the card will appear to lag behind the mouse because the position will be updated after drawing the sprite. Try it, if you want! Maybe you will like the effect.

Our object drag controller is now finished, but we may notice that, currently, `global.card` will always hold the value **noone**. We need to add some code that allows us to pick up a card by assigning its id to the `global.card` variable. But first, we need to add some code that assigns a random card color to each card instance. Let's handle that code inside of our card object. Open up the card object and add a new **Create Event** and an **Execute Code Action**.

**obj_card: Create Event**

```
/// Initialize the card object and choose a sprite
sprite_index=choose(spr_card_red,spr_card_green, spr_card_blue);
```

This line of code chooses a random card sprite from the ones that we have created and assigns it to our card. With this event out of the way, we are ready to add the code that picks up the card. Add a new event. This time we are going to choose the **Mouse, Left Pressed Event**.

**obj_card: Left Pressed Event**

```
/// Pick up the card
global.card=id;
depth=-1;
```

Now we can pick up the cards! It is as easy as assigning the id of the card instance that we clicked on to the global variable that we created in the drag controller object. Once we have done that, the drag controller object that we already coded takes care of the rest and moves the card around for us. We are also setting the depth to -1 to bring the card in front of other cards that may be in the room.

46

It's time to write the code that will allow us to drop cards. Add a new mouse event with a **Code Action**. With this one, we will use the **Mouse, Left Released Event**.

**obj_card: Left Released Event**

```
/// Drop the card on the ground or on the deck
var mx=mouse_x;
var my=mouse_y;
if (position_meeting(mx,my,obj_deck)) {
        // Add the card to the deck stack
        with (obj_deck) {
                ds_stack_push(deck,global.card.sprite_index);
        }

        // Destroy the card instance
        with (global.card) {
                instance_destroy();
        }
}
global.card=noone;
depth=0;
```

That is one of the most complicated sections of this example, so let me explain it. First, we get local references to the `mouse_x` and `mouse_y` positions. After that, we check to see if the mouse is hovering over the deck. If it is hovering over the deck, we push the `global.card` sprite index to the stack. For this example, we really only need to know what sprite the object had. After pushing to the stack, we destroy the card object. Once all of these steps have been executed, we set the `global.card` back to **noone** and set the depth back to zero. Of course, if the mouse isn't hovering over the deck, then we will ONLY set `global.card` to **noone** and set the depth to zero. This will drop the card on the ground, where we can pick it up again later.

Great job so far! There is only one more thing for us to add to get our game working. We need to allow the player to take a card off the top of the deck. Open up the deck object again and add a **Mouse, Left Pressed Event** to it. Drag a **Code Action** over into the event and write this code:

47

## obj_deck: Left Pressed Event

```
/// Remove the card from the deck
if (ds_stack_size(deck)>0) {
        var top_card=instance_create(x,y,obj_card);
        var card_sprite=ds_stack_pop(deck);
        top_card.sprite_index=card_sprite;
        global.card=top_card;
        global.card.depth=-1;
}
```

This last block of code is probably the second most complicated. The first thing we do is check to make sure that the stack isn't empty. If the stack is empty and we try to remove information from it, we would get bad information. Once we know for sure that the stack has information, we can continue. The next thing we do is create a new card instance and store it in a local variable called **top_card**. After that, we pop the sprite information that we stored in the stack and assign it to a local variable called **card_sprite**. Now, we have all of the information we need. We assign **card_sprite** to the new card instance that we created, make that new card instance **global.card**, and set its depth to -1 to simulate picking it up.

Congratulations! You just built a simple card game using a stack data structure. As you play around with the game, pay close attention to the order in which cards are removed from the deck. If you are perceptive, you will notice that cards are removed in the reverse order that they were placed in the deck. This example shows the main principles of how a stack works.

## Queues

A *queue* is a first-in-first-out (FIFO) data structure. The first data element that you add to it will be the first one that you can remove from it. The easiest way to understand a queue is just to think of a line at the supermarket. The first person in line will be the first person to be helped. Here is an image to help you imagine how a queue works:

# First In, First Out (FIFO)

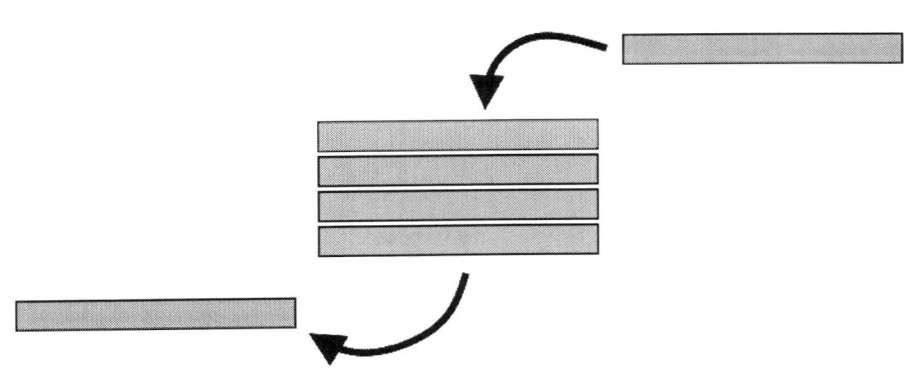

Let's create a queue. It's similar to how you would create a stack.

```
my_queue=ds_queue_create();
```

Create the queue and assign its id to a variable so that you can access it later.

You can destroy the queue like this:

```
ds_queue_destroy(my_queue);
```

To add an item to the queue, you use this function:

```
ds_queue_enqueue(my_queue,3);
```

To remove an item from the queue, you can use this function. It's a good idea to make sure the queue is not empty first.

```
if (!ds_queue_empty(my_queue)) {
        var number=ds_queue_dequeue(my_queue);
}
```

Queues have two ends; they have what is called the head of the queue and the tail of the queue. The head is the next value to be removed when using the **ds_queue_dequque** function. The tail is the last value added using the **ds_queue_enqueue** function. You can peek at the head or the tail without removing them using these functions:

```
var number=ds_queue_head(my_queue);
var number=ds_queue_tail(my_queue);
```

You can clear queues, copy queues, and find out how many values a queue contains, similar to how you did with the stack data structure.

```
ds_queue_clear(my_queue);

my_newqueue=ds_queue_create();
ds_queue_copy(my_newqueue,my_queue);

var queue_size=ds_queue_size(my_queue);
```

## Lists

The *list* data structure in GameMaker has quite a few different functions that the other structures you have seen so far do not have. Creating a list is very similar to creating a 1d array. However, one of the differences between lists and arrays is that you do not need to know how long a list is going to be. Using the same analogy used with arrays, boxes of data are added to the list dynamically, and so, you don't have to worry about the list's size when you create it.

```
my_list=ds_list_create();
```

Just like the other data structures, a list should be destroyed when it is no longer being used. They are easy to destroy. Use this simple function:

```
ds_list_destroy(my_list);
```

Below is the function that you can use to add a value to the list. The value will be added to the end of the list. The first argument in this function indicates the list that you are adding to, and the second argument (in this case, the number 3) is the value being added to the list.

```
ds_list_add(my_list,3);
```

The function below will delete a value from the list. Unlike with adding a value, the second argument is the index of the value that you would like to delete, not the value itself. Just like arrays, when you are trying to access a value in a list, you will need to use the index of the value.

```
ds_list_delete(my_list,0); // This function requires an index
```

Remember how when you add a value to a list, the new box is dynamically added? Well, the same is true in reverse. When you delete an item from the list, the box is dynamically removed and any boxes after the one removed will shift to take up the empty space. For example, if you remove the 6th item, and there is a 7th item, the 7th item will become the new 6th item.

Using the **ds_list_find_index** function, you provide a value and find its index (below, 3 is the value, not the index). If there are several items in the list that are the same, then this function will return the index of one of them, but you cannot know which one that it will return. If the value doesn't exist, this function will return a value of -1.

```
index=ds_list_find_index(my_list,3);
```

The `ds_list_find_value` function will return the value for the given index. This function will not remove the value from the list (which the pop function *will* do for a stack).

```
value=ds_list_find_value(my_list,0);
```

One of the cool things about the list data structure is that you can insert a value into the list and the other values will move out of the way, instead of being replaced. Below is the function you can use for that. The second argument is the index and the third argument is the value you would like to insert.

```
ds_list_insert(my_list,0,5);
```

If replacing the value is your actual goal, you can use the function below. Once again, the second argument is the index and the third is the value.

```
ds_list_replace(my_list,0,3);
```

List data structures have an easy-to-use, built-in shuffle function. This function could be useful for a card game.

```
ds_list_shuffle(my_list);
```

You also have the ability to sort the values in a list. The second argument is a boolean value that determines whether the list should be sorted in ascending order.

```
ds_list_sort(my_list,true);
```

Here are the steps you would take to create a copy of a list that you have already created:

```
my_newlist=ds_list_create();
ds_list_copy(my_newlist,my_list);
```

In the end, lists are very similar to 1d arrays, but they have some extra functions and, therefore, are better suited to certain programming situations.

## Maps

Maps are a very powerful data structure. They are similar to an object that has no events or scripts. Maps contain key-value pairs, which means that you have a list of keys where each key has a value assigned to it. Here is a way you might visualize a key value pair:

```
"key" : "value"
```

Let's take a quick look at some data that you might store in a **ds_map**. Note, that this is not code and you can't add data to a **ds_map** like this. This is just an example to help you visualize how the data is organized.

```
"class" : "wizard"
"attack" : 25
"speed" : 18
"mana" : 37
```

Creating a map is easy; this kind of function should look familiar to you by now.

```
my_map=ds_map_create();
```

It is easy to clear a map of all of its key-value pairs. Be aware that this function doesn't actually destroy the map. It just clears the map of every key-value pair.

```
ds_map_clear(my_map);
```

The code below shows how to add a new key-value pair to the map. Be sure to check out the easier way to do this just a little later in the chapter where I talk about accessors.

```
ds_map_add(my_map,'hp',25);
```

The function below shows how you can actually destroy the map that was created. This should be done once you are done using a map.

```
ds_map_destroy(my_map);
```

Maps are a great way to store a large amount of data in an organized way. They are necessary when using the networking functions in GameMaker Language, so be sure to study them well.

## Grids

*Grids* are the last data structure that I will talk about in this book. Grids are exactly what they sound like. Imagine a chessboard where each square can hold some piece of information. You can create grids of any size and manipulate specific areas or squares inside the grid. Grids are similar to 2d arrays, but they have a few unique functions.

The function below shows how you can create a grid. The first argument is the number of columns, and the second argument is the number of rows. Let's create a grid with only 9 total cells.

```
my_grid=ds_grid_create(3,3);
```

And (really quickly) I'm going to show you how you can destroy a grid as well. Note that when you are done using the grid, you should call this function.

```
ds_grid_destroy(my_grid);
```

There are dozens of functions that you can use with grids. They are all super cool, and I would highly recommend learning about them. I'm going to cover a few of the main ones here, but I'm not going to talk about all of them, because the GameMaker Help file explains them all very well. After showing you the functions, we will build an example game using a grid so that you can learn about the practical applications that this data structure provides.

Let's start with the basics. After you have created the grid, you need to be able to add values to the cells. Below is the function you will use to set the values of individual cells. The first argument is the id of the grid, the second is the x position in the grid, the third is the y position, and the fourth is the value to be added.

```
ds_grid_set(my_grid,0,0,3);
```

It is also possible to set cell values on multiple cells. Below is the function you can use to set the cell values for a rectangular region. The first argument is the grid id again, the second and third are the x and y position, respectively, for the left corner of the rectangle. The fourth and fifth arguments are the x and y position, respectively, for the bottom right corner. Finally, the sixth argument is the the value that will be set for each cell inside the region.

```
ds_grid_set_region(my_grid,0,0,2,2,3);
```

It is also possible to set a region that has a circular shape (called a "disk" by GameMaker). You will have to check the help file for more information on that one though.

Next, I'm going to show you how you can retrieve a value from the grid. Below is the function that you will use. The first argument is the id, the second is the x position of the cell, and the third is the y position of the cell.

```
var num=ds_grid_get(my_grid,0,0);
```

This piece of code will retrieve the value from the upper-left cell in the grid and store it in the local variable **num**.

Now that you have a solid, basic understanding of this data structure, let's create a real game example together to help you get more comfortable with these functions.

## Tic-Tac-Toe with a Grid Data Structure

Let's step through a very simple example of how we can set up and use a grid to make a Tic-tac-toe game in GameMaker.

The first thing that we need to do for this example is create a new sprite and name it **spr_char**. This sprite will have a width of 160, a height of 160 (these two numbers will set the size of each cell in the grid), an x origin of zero, and a y origin of zero. It will also have two subimages. The first subimage will be a giant circle or "O" and the second subimage will be a giant cross or "X".

The second thing we will need is a new background called **bg_tiles**. We are going to use this background to create the 9 squares needed in every

Tic-tac-toe game. Give this background a width and a height of 160. Leave the center of the background transparent, but draw a white outline around all four edges.

After creating the sprite and the background, create a new object and name it **obj_game**. This will be the only object in our example. It will contain our grid data structure and all of the code that is required to run the game. Add a new `Create Event` to the object.

**obj_game: Create Event**

```
/// Create the ds_grid and initialize the
// game object
grid=ds_grid_create(3,3);
ds_grid_set_region(grid,0,0,2,2,-1);
```

This code creates a new grid and then sets every grid square equal to -1. The arguments for **ds_grid_set_region** should be explained. The first argument is the id of the grid. The next two arguments are the x and y position, respectively, for the upper-left corner of the region, followed by the two arguments for the x and y position, respectively, for the lower-right corner of the region. The last argument is the value that should be set for each square or cell in the region. For our example, we will use -1 to represent an empty cell, 0 to represent an "O" cell, and 1 to represent an "X" cell. If you are extra perceptive, you will notice the "O" subimage in our sprite has an **image_index** of 0 and the "X" subimage in our sprite has an **image_index** of 1. We will be using this fact to our advantage.

It's time for the next phase in our Tic-tac-toe example. Add a new `Mouse > Global > Global Left Pressed` Event and drag over a `Code Action`. Inside the `Code Action`, type this code:

**obj_game: Global Left Pressed**

```
/// Set an O
var gridx=mouse_x div 160;
var gridy=mouse_y div 160;
ds_grid_set(grid,gridx,gridy,0);
```

57

This small code will set an "O" at the clicked cell location in the grid. The `ds_grid_set` function takes a grid id as its first argument, the x value as its second argument, the y value as its third argument, and the value that the cell will be set to as its fourth argument. Here, we are setting the value to 0, which is our digital representation of "O".

Before we move on, it is important to have a small discussion about the math involved here. We have decided that our room should be divided up into 9 squares, each square being 160 pixels wide and 160 pixels tall. The upper-left of our square in the room could have x values and y values anywhere from 0 to 159, but in our grid, the x and y values of the upper-left square will both be 0. Our middle square in the room could have x and y values anywhere from 160 to 319, but in our grid, the x and y values will both be 1.

We need some way to convert from the range of values in the room to the single value in the grid. One way to do this is to divide the x and y mouse positions from the room by the grid cell size (160) and then round them down (using the floor function). This works well, but there is an easier way. GameMaker has an operator called the `div` operator. This operator takes two operands, divides them, and returns a whole number answer (meaning that it doesn't have the remainder). The `mod` operator and the `div` operator are very similar. The difference is that the `mod` operator returns only the remainder, without the whole number answer. Using this cool math trick, we can calculate the grid x and y values of the mouse's x and y positions in the room. Just as a side note, we can also use this method to make objects snap to a grid.

Now that the math is out of the way, we need to add a way for our player to place an "X" in the room. The code will be similar to that for setting an "O", but we will put it in a **Mouse > Global Mouse > Global Right Pressed Event**.

**obj_game: Global Right Pressed**

```
/// Set an X
var gridx=mouse_x div 160;
```

```
var gridy=mouse_y div 160;
ds_grid_set(grid,gridx,gridy,1);
```

We are setting the grid value to 1, because that is the digital representation that we chose for "X".

The last piece that we need in order to finish our small Tic-tac-toe grid example is the code that will draw our game. This code can get a little tricky, because we need to have one *for loop* nested inside another for loop. I'll do my best to explain it.

**obj_game: Draw Event**

```
/// Draw the grid
var gridw=ds_grid_width(grid);
var gridh=ds_grid_height(grid);
for (var i=0; i<gridw; i++) {
        for (var j=0; j<gridh; j++) {
                if(ds_grid_get(grid,j,i)==-1) {
                        continue;
                }
                var subi=ds_grid_get(grid,j,i);
                draw_sprite(spr_char, subi,j*160,i*160);
        }
}
```

The two for loops in this code are used to cycle through the different cells in our grid. `j` represents the x values and `i` represents the y values. In each cell, we check its value. If the value is equal to -1, we continue (jump out of this current loop and start the next iteration). If it doesn't equal -1, we will draw a sprite with an `image_index` of the value found in the grid. We will need to multiply the x and y positions in the grid by 160 to convert them from grid values to room x and y positions.

Now, create a new room, give it a name, a width of 480, and a height of 480. Click the backgrounds tab, check "Visible when room starts", choose **bg_tiles** as the background, and make sure "Tile Hor." and "Tile Vert." are checked. We should see the classic Tic-tac-toe board in our room.

Click the objects tab and place **obj_game** in the room. Now, run the game and test it. We should be able to place "O"s by left clicking and "X"s by right clicking. Now, grab a friend and enjoy a game of Tic-tac-toe!

## Data Structure Accessors

The set of different functions used to set and get values from data structures is rather large and, in my opinion, kind of a pain to use. Luckily for us, the newer versions of GameMaker have a neat little trick called *accessors*. Accessors allow you to manipulate the values of a data structure in a more intuitive way. Let's look at some code.

```
stats=ds_map_create();
ds_map_add(stats,"health",100);
ds_map_add(stats,"mana",50);
```

This bit of code creates a map with two key-value pairs: one for the health and one for the mana. It's a giant mess of code for what little it actually does. Let me show you how to do the exact same thing using the accessor for map data structures.

```
stats = ds_map_create();
stats[? "health"] = 100;
stats[? "mana"] = 100;
```

Of course, the other cool thing about accessor code is that it can be used to both set and get values from the data structure.

You may be thinking that the code above looks kind of like an array with a funny question mark at the start of it, right? That question mark tells the compiler what type of data structure it is dealing with. Each data structure has its own symbol to be used in the accessor. Here are the different symbols and their corresponding data structure types:

```
list[| ]
```

```
map[? ]
grid[# ]
```

Accessors are a great way to make your code easier both to understand and to write. As far as I know, there is no way to chain accessors in GameMaker Language right now (if you had a map inside another map and tried to chain the accessors to get a value two levels down), but hopefully this functionality will be added in a later version.

# Chapter 5
# Expressions and Operators

## Expressions
An *expression* is a combination of operators and operands. If you haven't learned a programming language before, that statement might sound alien to you. I'll explain it in this chapter, and you should find that it is pretty easy to understand. Let me show you some examples of statements. You've actually seen them before.

```
x=10;
```

Easy, right? I told you they would be familiar. Let me dissect this expression for you so that I can explain my earlier comments. The "**x**" and the "**10**" are the *operands* in this statement. They represent the data being *operated* on. The "**=**" is the *operator*. It is *operating* on the two operands. The single equals sign is called the assignment operator. This is because it *assigns* the right operand to the left operand. You will also notice there are two operands. That makes the assignment operator a *binary* operator. In most programming languages, there are *unary*, *binary*, and sometimes *ternary* operators.

## Equality vs Assignment
This is not a difficult concept, but it is one of the most frequent mistakes new programmers make in GameMaker. (I've made it before...) Luckily, GameMaker Language is very forgiving. Best practice is to know the difference between these two operators and use them in the correct places; this is **very** important if you want to learn other major programming language later. The easy way to remember them is to know that the

equality operator is the *question* and the assignment operator is the *statement*.

## Equality Operator

The *equality* operator is the question, "Is this variable equal to this value?" This operator is represented by two equals signs, ==, and is commonly combined with an if statement (for more information on if statements, see Chapter 6). Here is an example:

```
if (health==0) {
        instance_destroy();
}
```

GameMaker is smart enough to know that if you (mistakenly) use a single equals sign (the assignment operator), the code will still work; however, this will get you into big trouble later if you ever move on to other programming languages. I would highly recommend getting in the habit of using this operator correctly.

## Assignment Operator

The *assignment* operator is the statement, "This variable now has this value." This operator is represented by a single equals sign and is commonly used when initializing a variable. Here is an example:

```
health=100;
```

GameMaker will NOT allow you to use a double equals sign (the equality operator) here. You will get an error if you try this.

## Equality with other Operations

The equality operator can be combined with other operators. The operators commonly combined with it are the greater than, less than, and not operators. Below are some examples of how these can be combined.

63

The following example checks to see if the player's health is less than or equal to zero. This can be very useful when the player takes damage that would put his health in the negative.

```
if (health<=0) {
        // Do something
}
```

This example checks to see if the player's health is greater than or equal to 100. This can be useful for making sure a variable has not passed some maximum value.

```
if (health>=100) {
        // Do something
}
```

This example checks to make sure the player's health is not equal to 100.

```
if (health!=100) {
        // Do something
}
```

## Add Operator

The *add* operator has two main functions in GameMaker. The first is doing the math of adding numbers together. Here is a simple example:

```
/// Add two numbers using the add operator
var result=5+3;
```

Can you guess the value of result? Pretty easy, right?

64

The second function of the add operator is to concatenate (concatenate just means to link) string values together. You've seen this before in a previous chapter, but I'm going to throw down a quick example here as well.

```
/// Create a full name using the add operator
var space=" ";
var full_name="Benjamin"+space+"Anderson";
```

Can you imagine the result of this operation? The add operator one of the most common operators in GameMaker Language. It is simple to understand but very important.

## Subtract Operator

Unlike the add operator, the *subtract* operator cannot be used with strings; it will only be used with numbers. With numbers, it does the simple math that you would expect.

```
/// Use the subtract operator to subtract two numbers
var result=5-3; // Returns 2
```

This operator is straightforward. Just remember not to use it with strings.

## Multiply Operator

The *multiply* operator does just what you would expect. To multiply, simply use the asterisk, *, symbol. Here is an example:

```
/// Use the multiply operator to get the product of two numbers
var result=5*3; // Returns 15
```

Just as easy as the subtract operator, but still very useful.

## Divide Operator

The *divide* operator, just like the multiply operator, works just as you would expect. It uses a single slash, /, symbol. Here is a simple example:

```
// Use the multiply operator to get the answer to 15/3
var result=15/3; // Returns 5
```

Soon, I will explain the division operator. Don't get these two confused! The division operator works differently from the divide operator!

## Assignment with Operation

The assignment operator can also be combined with the other operators in this way:

```
hp+=10;
hp-=10;
hp*=2;
hp/=2;
```

Each of the previous statements are equivalent to the following corresponding statements.

```
hp=hp+10;
hp=hp-10;
hp=hp*2;
hp=hp/2;
```

The simple operator combinations can be used as shortcuts. You will see them used more often than their written-out counterparts.

## Increment and Decrement Operator
The increment and decrement operators are also shortcuts. They are very commonly used in for loops, but they can be used outside for loops as well.

```
level++;
level--;
```

These two previous statements are (more or less) equivalent to these corresponding statements:

```
level+=1;
level-=1;
```

You can actually change the order of the operation like this:

```
++level;
level++;
```

This last version gets a little more complicated, and I rarely use them like this. The difference is that if you put the operator before, then it will return the incremented value. If you put the operator after, it will return the value and then increment it.

## The Not Operator
The *not* operator is like a switch in GameMaker Language. It works basically the same in many other programming languages. If you have a value that is equal to true and use you the not operator, then that value will become false. Here is an example:

```
var falling=false;
falling=!falling;
```

67

In this example, the falling variable starts out as false. The second line uses the not operator to flip it from false to true. You might ask why you can't just set it to true, like this:

```
falling=true;
```

Well, the answer is that you can, but what if the value is already true? If the value is already true, then using the not operator will switch it to false. Basically, the above code allows you to *toggle* the variable's value from false to true or from true to false, and you don't have to know what it was originally. You just know that it is now the opposite of what it was before.

You can also use the not operator in condition statements. You have seen this in a previous section that talked about combining the equality operator with other operators.

## Division Operator

The *division* operator is different from the divide operator because it returns a whole number (that is, with no remainder). This is convenient because you can use this anytime that you need to calculate snapping to a grid.

**End Step Event**

```
/// Make an object follow the mouse while snapping to a 32x32 grid
x=(mouse_x div 32)*32;
y=(mouse_y div 32)*32;
```

In this code, you are using the division operator to get the whole-number value of the mouse position divided by 32. If the mouse position is 64, then the answer will be 2. If the mouse position is 67, then answer will still be 2. After you get the value, you multiply your answer by 32. As you can see, both cases (values of 64 and 67) will return 64.

The division operator is a little tricky at first, but once you figure it out, it can be very useful.

## Modulo Operator

The *modulo* operator is the complement to the division operator: instead of returning the whole-number answer, the modulo operator returns the remainder after performing the division. One common use for this is to discover whether a number is odd or even.

```
/// Use the modulo operator to find if a number is odd or even
var num=irandom(10);
var is_even=((num mod 2)==0);
```

As you can see, you use the modulo operator to divide **num** by 2. If the returned whole number remainder (the result of the operation) is equal to 0, then you know that the number is even. If not, the number must be odd.

The modulo operator is even trickier than the division operator, but it is also well worth the few minutes that it will take you to learn how to use it.

# Chapter 6
# Statements

## Control Statements

In programming, control statements are used to "branch" your code, meaning to run different sections of code based on a specific condition. The most basic form is an *if statement*.

## If

The *if* control statement is very important to programming in any language. It makes it possible to execute code based on a specified condition. Here is an example of when you might use an *if* statement in GameMaker Language:

```
if (keyboard_check(vk_right)) {
    x+=4;
}
```

This code will check to see if the keyboard's right arrow key is being pressed; if it is, then the code will add 4 to the current x position of the object that is running the code. Adding 4 to the current x position will move the object to the right on the screen.

Now that you have seen an in-game example of where you might use an if statement, let me show you a generic example.

```
if (condition) {
    statement;
}
```

If statements are fairly easy to understand, even for new programmers. The thing you need to check carefully is where you want your curly braces to end. Being consistent with your formatting style will help you to reduce bugs and make your code easier to read. Here are two common ways to format statements, starting with the one that I use most often.

### First Example

```
if (condition) {
        statement;
}
```

### Second Example

```
if (condition)
{
        statement;
}
```

It really doesn't matter which method you choose to use (the compiler treats these as equivalent), or if you choose to use one that I don't have listed here. What **really** matters is that you choose one style and then stick with it. You will have **way** fewer bugs if you are consistent.

## Else

The *else* control statement goes right along with the if control statement. The else is what happens if the condition inside the if evaluates to false.

```
if (condition) {
        // True? Do this statement
} else {
        // False? Do this statement
}
```

## Else if

The *else if* control statement is also combined with the if control statement. You can chain else if as many times as is necessary to build the logical structure that you want to use.

```
if (condition1) {
        // Condition1 is true? Do this
     // statement
} else if (condition2) {
        // Condition2 is true? Do this
     // statement
} else if (condition3) {
        // Condition3 is true? Do this
     // statement
} else {
        // None are true? Do this statement
}
```

## Switch

The *switch* control statement is an alternative to the if / else if / else combination.

```
switch (expression) {
        case value1:
                // Does expression evaluate to
            // value1? Do this
                break;
        case value2:
                // Does expression evaluate to
            // value2? Do this
                break;
        default:
                // Do this if none are true
                break;
}
```

This one is a little tricky to understand with a generic example like this. An in-game use would better explain it.

72

```
switch(direction) {
        case 0:
                // We are moving to the right
                sprite_index=spr_player_right;
                break;
        case 90:
                // We are moving up
                sprite_index=spr_player_up;
                break;
        case 180:
                // We are moving to the left
                sprite_index=spr_player_left;
                break;
        case 270:
                // We are moving down
                sprite_index=spr_player_down;
                break;
        default:
                // We are moving at an angle
                // Do nothing
                break;
}
```

This switch statement checks if an object is moving right, left, up, or down, and changes the sprite accordingly. The **break** statement at the end of each **case** prevents the **switch** statement from checking the other cases as well.

## With

*With* is a powerful control statement inside GameMaker that allows you to run some code in the context of another object. An example will explain this best.

```
// Code inside the enemy object
with (obj_player) {
        hp-=10;
}
```

Even though this code is run from inside the enemy object, it is actually subtracting health from the player object and not from itself. You can also do this using the dot operator.

```
// Code inside the enemy object
obj_player.hp-=10;
```

This is basically the same thing but the with control statement is useful when you need to perform tons of changes on the other object, because you don't have to keep referencing the object; you only reference it once. One other difference is that if you want to call a function inside the player object, you *must* use the with statement; you can't use the dot operator.

## Loop Statements

*Loop statements* in GameMaker Language allow you to run a line of code multiple times with slight differences. This is important for many kinds of games. There are four main loop statements that can be used in GameMaker, and there are different reasons for choosing each one.

## Repeat

*Repeat* is the shortest and the simplest of all of the loops. It allows you to run the same section of code multiple times in a single **Step Event** (which happens basically instantaneously during runtime).

```
repeat (10) {
        var rand_x = random(room_width);
        var rand_y = random(room_height);
        instance_create(rand_x,rand_y,obj_enemy);
}
```

This code will create ten enemies in random locations throughout the room. Of course, instead, you could type the **instance_create()** function out ten times, but that would be a pain.

74

## While

The *while* loop is a little more complicated than the repeat loop, but it's not too bad either. The while loop takes a condition, and, if the condition is true, will repeat all the code within its curly braces. Once the condition is false, the while loop will exit.

## For

The *for* loop is probably the hardest to understand out of all of the control statements, but it is powerful, and you need to know how it works.

```
for (var i=0; i<10; i++) {
        draw_line(32*i,0,32*i,room_height);
}
```

Let me first tell you what this code does, and then I will explain how it does it. This code draws vertical lines stretching the entire height of the room. The first line is drawn at an x position of 32, and each line after that adds another 32 to the x position.

The first part of the for loop you need to understand is the part wrapped in parenthesis.

```
for (var i=0; i<10; i++)
```

This part is made up of 3 sections. The first section is the initialization section, the second is the condition section, and the third is the iteration section.

```
for (initialize; condition; iterate)
```

The initialize section is only run the first time. It is generally used to create the variable that you will be using to iterate and check against in the condition. The condition section is checked every loop. If the condition evaluates to true, then the loop will run again. If the condition evaluates to

75

false, then the loop will not run again. The iteration section is run every time the condition section evaluates to true, but after the code itself has been run.

I know this will be a little bit confusing if for loops are new to you. Let's step through a short loop.

```
for (var i=0; i<2; i++) {
        show_message("Hi");
}
```

This for loop will first create the variable i and set it to 0. After that, it will check to see if i is less than 2; because it is less than 2, the **show_message** code will be run. Then, the iteration section will be run and i++ will add 1 to i, making it now equal to 1. The condition section will make sure that i is still less than 2. Because i is equal to 1, the loop will evaluate as true and the **show_message** code will be run again. Now, the i++ code will run again, setting i to 2. The condition section will check if i is less than 2; since it is no longer less than 2, the **show_message** code will NOT be run again, and the program will exit the loop.

Hopefully, that small example helped. Be sure to watch my video about for loops if you are still struggling with them.

## Expression Statements
Here are a few common expression statements that you will find useful.

### Return
*Return* statements are most useful in scripts. For example, you might create a script like this:

```
///scr_add(n1,n2);
return argument[0]+argument[1];
```

76

You might not understand all of what is going on here, but know that this script takes two arguments (values) and then *returns* their sum. After creating this script, you could call it like this:

```
sum=scr_add(5,7); // sum now holds the value 12
```

As you can see, the script returns the number that has been added together inside the script. Many GameMaker functions return values, and it's very important to understand what value types are returned from them.

## Break

*Break* is commonly used in switch statements, but it can also be used in other loop statements to break out of the loop.

```
for(var i=0; i<100; i++) {
    // Some code
        if (i==9) break;
}
```

That is a simple for loop. In a normal situation, it will run the code inside the loop 100 times; however, once i reaches 9, it will call the **break** statement and exit the loop, running only 10 times.

Break statements elsewhere will also exit the loop once they are reached by the compiler. This means that every line of code before the break will be run inside that loop, and every line after it will not be run.

Break statements will exit out of for loops, while loops, repeat loops, and with statements.

## Continue

The *continue* statement works similarly to the break statement, but instead of exiting out of the loop completely, it simply skips one iteration. Basically, there may be times when you wish to skip one specific step in the loop but continue to execute the rest of the steps in the loop.

## Exit

Exit works like the break statement, but it applies to the entire section of code. If you place an exit in a script, it will exit the script completely. If you put one in a `Code Action`, it will exit that entire action (not the event, but the action).

# Chapter 7
# Scripts

## Creating Scripts

Scripts are amazing! They are also easy to use! If you have ever programmed in a different language, a *script* is similar to a function, in that it allows you to write a block of code once and then run that block of code multiple times by executing the script it is contained in. One of the interesting things about scripts is that they are global in scope. When I say global, I mean that if you create a script, any object in your game **could** call that script. If you see lots of repeated code in your game, then it might be a good idea to create a script for that code and then just call the script whenever needed.

Creating a script is pretty easy. You can use the shortcut keys shift+ctrl+c to add a new script to your game, or you can click the page icon with the green play symbol on it. After adding a new script, you will need to give the script its own identifier. Scripts, just like variables, have an identifier. Let's create a script called `scr_move_right`. I'm going to put the name (identifier) of the script at the upper left-hand side of the code block so that you know it is a script and you know what it is called.

`scr_move_right`

```
/// scr_move_right()
x+=4;
```

As stated before, the `scr_move_right` on the upper left-hand side of the code block is the actual identifier for the script. In GameMaker, you will place the identifier for the script in this location. The triple slash comment has a special meaning at the top of a script file, as I described in Chapter 1. This comment provides the auto-complete functionality in GameMaker and can also be used to tell you the order of arguments that need to be passed to the script. The last line in the script simply moves the player four pixels to the right. This basic script isn't super useful, but let me show you one that I use quite often in my projects.

**scr_get_depth**

```
///scr_get_depth()
depth=-y;
```

This is a neat little script that will give objects that are closer to the bottom of the screen a lower depth (meaning that they will be drawn on top of objects that are closer to the top of the screen). This gives the game a sense of depth and, when used correctly, can create a cool visual effect.

## Script Arguments

Just like functions, scripts can be passed arguments. Let's upgrade the script we wrote in the last section from **scr_move_right** to **scr_move** and pass it some arguments.

**scr_move**

```
/// scr_move(xmov,ymov)
x+=argument[0];
y+=argument[1];
```

There is an array in the local scope of each script called **argument**. It contains the values of the arguments that were passed to the script in the order in which they were passed. The first value passed in will be assigned to **argument[0]**, the second to **argument[1]**, and so on.

I usually assign these values to local variables in order to help with the readability of the script.

**scr_move**

```
/// scr_move(xmov,ymov)
var xmov=argument[0];
var ymov=argument[1];
```

80

```
x+=xmov;
y+=ymov;
```

It may seem a little redundant in this particular script (and maybe it is), but in a script where the argument is being used in multiple places, it is easier to understand a named variable than the generic `argument[0]`.

## Scripts Return Values

Scripts can also return a value. This means that you can pass data to the script, do something with that data to get a result, and then have that result pop back out. For example, you might create a script like this.

**scr_add**

```
///scr_add(n1,n2);
return argument[0]+argument[1];
```

You might not understand all of what is going on here, but know that this script takes two arguments (values) and then *returns* the sum. After creating this script, you could call it like this:

**obj_add_button: Mouse Pressed Event**

```
sum=scr_add(5,7); // sum now holds the value 12
```

As you can see, this script will actually return the result of the two arguments added together by the script.

## Executing Scripts

Let me show you how you can call a script inside your code. There are two ways to do so. The easiest way is to write the identifier for the script followed closely by two parenthesis. These two parenthesis are called the *script call operator*; they will cause the script to be executed.

```
scr_get_depth();
```

Let's look at the second way you can call a script. This way involves a new function inside GameMaker Language called the **execute_script** function. Make sure that when you pass the script into this function you do not add the brackets to the end.

```
execute_script(scr_get_depth);
```

Now, you might be wondering why on earth you would ever use this when it takes longer to type. The benefit of this method is that you can run a script that has been assigned to a variable.

```
var my_script = scr_get_depth;
execute_script(my_script);
```

This is useful when you have a parent object that runs different scripts for each of its child objects (see chapter 8 for more information on the child/parent relationship in objects) depending on what you want them to do. Make sure that you don't use the script call operator when assigning the script to a variable or executing it inside the **execute_script** function.

Also, note that when you assign a script to a variable (as seen in the code above) you do not use the brackets on the end of the script. The brackets represents the script call operator or function call operator; therefore, they would cause GameMaker to execute the script and attempt to assign its returned value to the variable, instead of assigning the script's id to the variable.

This chapter on scripts has been short and sweet, but hopefully you learned something from it that you can apply in your future projects. I love using scripts to help organize my code, and I hope that you can find them useful as well.

# Chapter 8
# Objects and Sprites

## Creating Object Instances
Something that I didn't pick up on right away when I first started using GameMaker is the difference between instances and objects.

An object in GameMaker is kind of like a cookie cutter, whereas the instance is sort of like the cookie. Objects are used as the molds for creating instances.

There are two ways to create an instance of an object in GameMaker. The first way is to simply place the instance in a room. This creates a new instance of the object that you have selected.

The other way to create a new instance of an object is by using the **instance_create** function. It is a simple function that takes only 3 arguments.

```
instance_create(32,32,obj_player);
```

This line of code will create an instance of the player object at x position 32, y position 32.

## Object Properties
Every instance created from an object starts off with some basic properties. These properties are built-in variables, which have their own default values, and identifiers. There are quite a few of these properties, but let's start off with the basics.

## Basic Instance Properties

`id`

An instance's *id* is represented by a real value, in other words, a number. You can store this number in a variable that can later be used to refer to the instance. You will find an instance's id can be your best friend.

`solid`

Even though GameMaker has a built-in **solid** boolean property, I wouldn't recommend using it. This variable affects the way GameMaker handles the **Collision Event**, and often, the effect is not a great one. The best way I've found to handle collisions is using a parent object. I'll show you more about this later.

`visible`

The **visible** instance property is a simple boolean property that determines whether the instance is drawn on the screen or not.

`persistent`

The **persistent** property is another boolean property that determines whether the instance is carried over between rooms. If persistent is set to true, then the instance will not be destroyed when changing rooms; it will also retain the values of all of its other properties.

`depth`

The **depth** property is necessary. This property can be any real integer value. It controls which objects are drawn in front of other objects. Lower values are brought to the front and higher values are pushed to the back. If you have a tree object that you want to be in the background (behind the player), you might give it a depth value of -5 and your player a depth value of -10. This would draw the player object in front of the tree object because -10 is *lower* than -5.

```
alarm
```

The **alarm** property is an array that is used in conjunction with alarm events. The property **alarm[0]** would return the value of the Alarm 0 event.

```
object_index
```

The **object_index** property returns a real value representing the id of that object (not the instance). This property can be used to compare instances to see if they were created from the same object.

```
x
```

The **x** property represents the current x position of the instance.

```
y
```

The **y** property represents the current y position of the instance.

```
xstart
```

The **xstart** property is the x position of the instance at the moment when it was created.

```
ystart
```

The **ystart** property is the y position of the instance at the moment when it was created.

```
xprevious
```

The **xprevious** property is the x position of the instance in the previous step.

```
yprevious
```

The **yprevious** property is the y position of the instance in the previous step.

```
direction
```

The **direction** property is the direction in which the instance will move if the **speed** property is set. It uses degrees, and it defaults to 0.

```
speed
```

The **speed** property is the speed at which the instance will move. If the **direction** property is not set, then the instance will move to the right.

```
friction
```

The **friction** property is a value that gets subtracted from the **speed** property at every step. If you have a speed of 10 and a friction of 1, then it will take 10 steps for the speed to fall to zero.

```
hspeed
```

The **hspeed** property represents the horizontal speed of the instance. A positive number will move the instance to the **right**, and a negative number will move the instance to the **left**.

```
vspeed
```

The **vspeed** property represents the vertical speed of the instance. A positive number will move the instance **down**, and a negative number will move the instance **up**.

## Sprite Instance Properties
The sprite instance properties are a set of properties that are used to control the sprite associated with a particular instance.

`sprite_index`

The `sprite_index` property can be used to get or set the sprite associated with an instance. It is generally used to change the sprite of an instance.

`image_index`

The `image_index` represents the animation subimage index. If you have an animation with five subimages, and you want to set it to the first one, you would set `image_index` to 0.

`image_speed`

The `image_speed` property controls the speed at which the sprite animates, or more specifically, the speed at which it cycles through its subimages.

`image_count`

The `image_count` property returns the number of subimages in the sprite associated with the instance. Note that this returns the number, not the value. The last subimage will actually be 1 less than `image_count` because the subimage index starts at 0.

## Object Inheritance

Object inheritance is one of my favorite features of GameMaker. A solid understanding of this section is very helpful if you ever want to build a large-scale project like a role-playing game because it allows you to reuse code in objects that will have similar behaviors. The first thing that you need to know is how to set up object inheritance and what the common terms are.

## Setting up Inheritance

You can make one object inherit events and certain properties from another with GameMaker's inheritance system. GameMaker uses the terms parent and child to describe the inheritance relationship between objects. The *child* object will inherit events and certain properties from its *parent* object. I'll describe the specifics of how that works a little later, but for now, let's look at how you can set up this relationship.

When you open up one of your objects from the resource tree, you will see a property next to the mask property labelled "parent." Click on that property and select the object that you want to become this object's parent. You cannot select the same object, as this would create a loop.

Once the parent/child relationship has been set, the child object will inherit events from the parent object. There are some important rules that you should be made aware of regarding how the inheritance actually works.

1. Child objects **will** inherit events from grandparents, great grandparents, and so on (see second rule for exceptions).
2. Child objects **will not** inherit events that they possess themselves.
3. It is possible for child events to have their own event and still run the parent's event using the `events_inherited()` function.

Let's talk about rule three a little, because it is especially important. There will be cases when you want to create a base parent object and have children execute the base events of the parent, but also contain their own unique additions to the event.

Generally, when I start creating a new game, I try to think about the main objects in my game and what actions they will be performing. After I figure these two things out, I start separating those actions into two categories, **actions that will be the same** between objects and **actions that will be different**. Let me give you a quick example.

You are building a platform game. You have two main types of objects. You have your player object, and you have your enemy objects. You want

90

the player object and the enemy objects to be able to interact with the world in the normal platformer type way (falling, running, jumping, and such). You want your player object to be able to shoot arrows at the enemies, and you want the enemies to shoot fireballs at the player.

Step one is to separate the actions that will be the same and the actions that will be different (there are many good ways to set this up, I'm only going to show you one of them).

## Actions that will be the same
1. Gravity
2. Jumping
3. Collisions

## Actions that will be different
1. Input (user controls player, AI controls enemy)
2. Attacking (enemy shoots fire, player shoots arrows)

Once you have the actions separated, it is time to create your objects. You will create a **parent** object that controls the **actions that are the same** and then two **child** objects that will add to the parent's actions and **control the actions that are different**.

If you are new to programming, you might be asking yourself why you would do this. The answer is that it will make your life easier later. Let's say that instead of using a parent object, you just coded the actions that will be the same twice, once for each child object. The code would work exactly the same, right? Also, you wouldn't have to worry about parent object logic. You would be right to make these assumptions. But what if, instead of having two children, you have 20? Then, you would have to write the same code 20 times. What if you still decided to just push through and write the code 20 times, but then later, you wanted to change it? You would have to change your code in 20 different places. This could cause errors and discrepancies. If you use a parent system, then you need to write the code only once and then, if need be, change it in only one place.

Getting used to the inheritance system in GameMaker can be tricky sometimes, but the effort is well worth the benefits. Once you get it down, it will become one of your favorite features of GameMaker Language.

## Identifying Instances

We've already talked about the differences between objects and instances. There are times in your programming where you will want to work with a specific instance. One way to do this is to create a reference to the instance at the time it's created. A common place for this is when an enemy fires a bullet at the player.

The `instance_create` function returns the id of the instance created. Because of this, we are able to create a reference to the instance like this:

```
// Creates a bullet instance
var bullet=instance_create(x,y,obj_bullet);
```

After we have created the instance and we have a reference to it, we can set its properties and have it call functions.

```
// Set the direction of the bullet instance
bullet.direction=dir;

// Call a script inside the bullet instance.
with (bullet) {
    scr_move();
}
```

This is all made possible because we have a variable as a reference to the instance.

If the instance has already been created, it is still possible to get a reference to it using some different functions. Let's look at a few of these different methods.

92

## The Nearest Object Instance

There is a useful little function in GameMaker that can be used to get the id of the nearest instance of an object. This function is called `instance_nearest`. Here is an example of how it works:

`obj_player`: Draw Event

```
// Get a reference to the id of the nearest enemy object
var near_enemy=instance_nearest(x,y,obj_enemy);
draw_sprite(spr_target,0,near_enemy.x,near_enemy.y);
```

The `instance_nearest` function returns the id of the instance that is nearest to the x and y position passed into the function. You can use this to store the id in a variable and then access it later. As you can see in the code above, we use the variable that contains the id of the nearest enemy object to draw a target sprite on it. This is one of the many uses that this function has.

## The Furthest Object Instance

There is also a function in GameMaker that is quite the opposite of `instance_nearest`. it is called `instance_furthest`. It takes the same arguments, but it will return the id of the instance that is farthest from the point given, instead of the nearest.

`obj_player`: Draw Event

```
// Get a reference to the id of the farthest enemy object
var far_enemy=instance_furthest(x,y,obj_enemy);
draw_sprite(spr_target,0,far_enemy.x,far_enemy.y);
```

This line of code will draw `spr_target` at the position of the enemy object that is the farthest from the player's x and y position.

# Instance at a Position

This is one of the most useful functions for getting a reference to an instance. You only need to know where that instance is, and you can use that information to get the id of the instance. Here is an example:

**obj_player: Step Event**

```
// Check to see if the left mouse button is being pressed
if (mouse_button_check(mb_left)) {

    // Find the enemy object at the mouse's position
    var i=instance_position(mouse_x,mouse_y,obj_enemy);

    // Destroy the found instance
    with (i) {
        instance_destroy();
    }
}
```

This bit of code checks to see if the user is pressing the mouse button. If they are, then it checks to see if there is an instance of the enemy object at that location. If there is, then it stores the id of that instance in the local variable "`i`". After that, it destroys the instance found.

# Instance at a Place

There is one last function that I think is worth mentioning here. I use this one less often, but it is also useful. It is called the `instance_place` function. This function works almost exactly like the `instance_position` function. It takes the same arguments and will also return the id of the instance found. The one major difference is that this function **uses the mask of the object calling and checks for a collision at the position passed**, whereas `instance_position` only checks the one-pixel point that is passed. This can cause drastic differences in results. Make sure that you understand this distinction when choosing between these two functions. I generally use `instance_position` more often.

**obj_player: Step Event**

```
// Check to see if the left mouse button is being pressed
```

94

```
if (mouse_button_check(mb_left)) {

        // Find the enemy object that would collide with the
        // player object if it were at the mouse's position
        var i=instance_place(mouse_x,mouse_y,obj_enemy);

        // Destroy the found instance
        with (i) {
                instance_destroy();
        }
}
```

Here is the same code as above, but using **instance_place** instead. I've added extra comments to help you to understand the difference between the two.

## No Instance Found

Now is a good time to mention what these functions will return if they can't find an instance of the object you are looking for. There is a special constant in GameMaker called **noone**. This constant represents no object. It has an actual value of -4. The code below shows how you might use this constant. I like to use it because it makes the code easier to read and understand.

```
var i=instance_position(mouse_x,mouse_y,obj_enemy);

// Make sure we actually found an instance before we
// attempt to destroy it.
if (i!=noone) {
        with (i) {
                instance_destroy();
        }
}
```

Once you get the hang of using all of these great properties and functions with objects and instances, you will see how sweet they are. There is a lot to learn here, but it is fun when you start to use these to add features to your game. In the Events chapter, I will talk about one more way that you can get access to a specific instance in the room, but you have learned quite a bit already.

# Chapter 9
# Events

## Events
In GameMaker Studio, each object has a list of events that can be fired (triggered) by instances of that object during the game.

### Create Event
The `Create Event` is only run when an instance is first created and then is never used again during the life of that instance. It is an important event for setting up default properties and variables.

### Step Events
The `Step Event` is run once at every frame of the game. If your game is set to run at 30 fps (frames per second), then your `Step Event` will be executed thirty times per second. This event is mainly used for controlling the states of your objects.

### Begin Step Event
The `Begin Step Event` is almost exactly like the `Step Event`; the only difference is that the `Begin Step Event` runs first. If you need to run a specific bit of code every game frame but want to run it before your `Step Event`, then this is the event for you.

### End Step Event
The `End Step Event` is also almost exactly like the `Step Event`; the difference here is that the `End Step Event` runs after the `Step Event`. This can be especially useful when having an object follow the mouse or another object. You will notice that if you make an object follow the mouse like this in the `Step Event`, there seems to be some lag.

Step Event

```
x=mouse_x;
y=mouse_y;
```

If you place the above code in the `End Step Event`, there will be no lag. This is due to the timing of the `End Step Event` coming after the `Draw Event`.

## Alarm Events

The `Alarm Event` works just like any alarm: you set a length of time for the alarm to wait and at the end of that time, something happens. Alarms are almost necessary in every game. Understanding of how alarms work should be obtained as quickly as possible. I am going to give you several examples of how alarms work and how you can use them in a game. Let's start with the most basic example.

Create Event

```
/// Set an alarm
alarm[0]=120;
```

Here, we have a `Create Event`, and we are setting the alarm to a value of 120. Alarms automatically subtract from their value at every step. If your game is running at 30 fps (frames per second), then the `Alarm Event` will fire after 4 seconds (120/30=4). You will notice that alarms are part of an alarm array. This gives you the option of using multiple alarms. `alarm[0]` is the first alarm. Currently, nothing will happen when this alarm reaches the end of its 120 steps; this is where the `Alarm Event` comes in. Inside the `Alarm Event`, we can define the actions that we want to happen when the alarm reaches zero.

Alarm 0 Event

```
/// Execute some action at the end of the alarm
show_message("Wake up, sleepy head.");
```

In the `Alarm Event`, we can drag over a `Code Action` and execute any kind of code that we want. As a simple joke, this code only shows a pop-up message telling the user to wake up. This alarm will only go off once. If you want the alarm to cycle and show this pop-up message every 120 steps, then we need to set the alarm again inside the `Alarm Event` like this.

`Alarm 0 Event`

```
/// Execute some action at the end of the alarm
show_message("Wake up, sleepy head.");
alarm[0]=120;
```

As you can see, the only difference between this `Alarm Event` and the other one is that this one will reset its own timer. This will cause the alarm to run multiple times at a 120-step interval.

## Collision Event

There are several different ways to simulate a collision in games. The simplest way is to check the distance from the object that you are trying to collide with. One of the nice things about GameMaker is that it has a built-in event for collisions that handles all of the tricky collision code behind the scenes. Before I give you an example, you should know that if you check the "Precise collision checking" checkbox in your sprite, the collision checking for any object using that sprite will be quite a bit slower than if you were to leave that checkbox unchecked. The reason for this slowing is that "Precise collision checking" has to spend extra time to check each pixel of the sprite and see if it is colliding with the other object. You may think that this is what you want for your game, but 99% of the time, you will actually want to leave "Precise collision checking" turned off, as it can cause glitches in your game when your image cycles through its different subimages. For the majority of the games you build, using a square collision box is actually going to work better.

One other thing that you should know is that the `Collision Event` has a built-in reference to the object being collided with. This reference has an identifier of **other**. Let's look at a quick example that illustrates what I mean.

## Collision Event

```
/// Destroy both objects in the collision
instance_destroy();
With (other) {
        instance_destroy();
}
```

This code example will destroy both objects in the collision. First, we destroy the object calling the **Collision Event**, and then, we destroy the other object in the collision using the **other** reference.

Well, now you know basically all that you need to know in order to use collision events in your game.

## Keyboard Events

A **Keyboard Event** is fired when a specific key is pressed and will continue to fire each step that the user holds that key down. There are quite a few different keys that you can choose from. Here is an example of how you might use keyboard events to create movement in a game.

### Keyboard Up Event

```
/// Move the object up
y-=4;
```

### Keyboard Right Event

```
/// Move the object to the right
x+=4;
```

### Keyboard Down Event

```
/// Move the object down
y+=4;
```

100

Keyboard Left Event

```
/// Move the object to the left
x-=4;
```

You could also write similar code in the **Step Event** using **keyboard_check**. Which method you choose to use is more a matter of style than anything else. Mostly, I use the **Step Event** with the **keyboard_check** function.

## Key Press Event

The **Key Press Event** works similarly to the **Key Event**, except that it only fires in the single step in which the keyboard key is pressed down.

## Key Release Event

The **Key Release Event** also works similarly to the **Key Event**, but it will only fire in the single step in which the keyboard key is released.

## Mouse Events

A **Mouse Event** is fired when the cursor is hovering over the collision box for the object calling the event and a specific mouse button is pressed, or, in other words, when the user clicks on the object containing the **Mouse Event**. The **Mouse Event** will continue to fire every step that the user holds down the mouse button that was pressed.

### Create Event

```
/// Set the size of the object
size=1;
```

### Mouse Left Event

```
/// Increase the size of the object
image_xscale=size;
image_yscale=size;
size+=0.25;
```

In this example, we have both a **Create Event** and a **Mouse Left Event**. First, we set the size of the object to 1 in the **Create Event**. Then, we use the **Mouse Left Event** to increase the size of the object. The size will only increase if the cursor is hovering over the object's collision box and the left mouse button is being pressed.

## Mouse Pressed Events

The **Mouse Pressed Event** is similar to the **Mouse Event**, except that it will only fire during the step in which the mouse button is pressed down. Here is a simple example:

**Mouse Left Pressed Event**

```
/// Destroy the instance
instance_destroy();
```

This bit of code destroys the instance that is clicked on.

## Mouse Released Events

The **Mouse Released Event** is also similar to the **Mouse Event**, except that it will only fire during the step in which the mouse button is released. Here is an example similar to the one in the last section. You will notice that in this example, you can click on the instance, but it won't be destroyed until you release the mouse button.

**Mouse Left Released Event**

```
/// Destroy the instance
instance_destroy();
```

Once again, in this bit of code, we destroy the instance clicked on, but only when the mouse button is released.

## Global Mouse Events

A `Global Mouse Event` is fired when a mouse button is pressed, regardless of where the cursor is located in the game. The event also continues to fire in each step as long as the user holds down the mouse button. Here is a slightly larger example that shows how to use the `Alarm Event` with the `Global Mouse Left Pressed Event` for a neat bullet firing system in a game.

## Alarms and Global Left Pressed for Firing Bullets

Here is a combination of the `Global Left Pressed Event` and an `Alarm Event` to create a bullet firing system. A common use for alarms is to help with the timing of firing bullets in a game. In most games, we want the player to be able to hold the fire button down with fully automatic weapons, but we do not want the game to fire a bullet at every step, as this would be way too many bullets. We can limit the fire rate of our guns using alarms.

**Create Event**

```
/// Initialize the alarm
alarm[0]=-1;
fire_delay=8;
```

**Alarm 0 Event**

```
/// We only have this here so that the compiler doesn't remove the
// alarm event
```

**Global Left Pressed Event**

```
/// Fire the gun
if (alarm[0]==-1) {
        instance_create(x,y,obj_bullet);
        alarm[0]=fire_delay;
}
```

I'm throwing all the code down at once, and I'll explain it all here because it isn't very much code to explain. First, we add a `Create Event` where we set the alarm to -1 (its ending value), create the `fire_delay` variable and set it to 8. Next, we create the `Alarm 0 Event` and add a comment in it to make sure that the compiler doesn't remove the event. Finally, we add a `Global Left Pressed Event` where we check the value of the alarm, and then, create the bullet object if the value is equal to -1. After that, we make sure to reset the alarm to the `fire_delay` value so that the bullet will wait to be created until the alarm reaches a value of -1 again.

## Global Mouse Pressed Events

The `Global Mouse Pressed Event` works similarly to the `Global Mouse Event`, except that it only fires in the single step in which the mouse button is pressed down.

## Global Mouse Released Events

The `Global Mouse Released Event` also works similarly to the `Global Mouse Event`, except that it only fires in the single step in which the mouse button is released.

## Other Events

There are several different events that have been placed in the `Other Event` submenu. I will cover them here. Most will be easy for you to understand at a glance, and so, will have rather short explanations.

## Outside Room Event

The `Outside Room Event` fires once an object leaves the boundaries of the room. It continues to fire every step as long as the object stays outside the room.

## Intersect Boundary Event

The `Intersect Boundary Event` fires when an object intersects the boundary of the room. This means that if the object leaves the boundaries of the room, the event will fire and if the object returns to the boundaries of the room, the event will fire. In other words, this event fires once when it leaves and once when it returns.

## Outside View Event

The `Outside View Event` fires when an object leaves the boundaries of the view and continues to fire each step in which the object remains outside the boundaries of the view.

## Boundary View Event

The `Boundary View Event` fires when an object leaves the boundaries of a view and when the object returns to within the boundaries of a view. It works like the `Intersect Boundary Event` but with views instead of the room.

## Game Start Event

The `Game Start Event` only fires when the game is launched and at no other time during the game.

## Game End Event

The `Game End Event` only fires when the game ends and at no other time during the game.

## Room Start Event

The `Room Start Event` will fire at the start of each room.

## Room End Event

The `Room End Event` will fire at the end of each room.

## No More Lives Event

The `No More Lives Event` will fire if you are using GameMaker's built-in, global lives variable and the variable reaches 0.

## No More Health Event

The `No More Health Event` will fire if you are using GameMaker's built-in, global health variable and the variable reaches 0.

## Animation End Event

The `Animation End Event` fires when an object's sprite animation loop reaches the last subimage.

## End of Path Event

The `End of Path Event` fires if an object is moving along a path and it reaches the end of that path.

## User-Defined Event

User-defined events fire when the user fires them. They can be fired anywhere in your code using the `event_user` function. Here is an example of how you can do this.

**User Defined Event 0**

```
/// Show a message
show_message("This is my own event");
```

**Create Event**

```
/// Execute the user-defined event
var event_number=0;
event_user(event_number);
```

We start by creating the `User Defined Event`. For the sake of this example, I'm just showing a message. After, we call the event using `event_user`. We chose to use event number 0, and so, we pass that into the `event_user` function so that GameMaker knows which user event to fire. There are 16 user events that can be used.

## Draw Event

The `Draw Event` fires each step of the game, just like the `Step Event`. It is a good idea to put as little code in the `Draw Event` as possible. You should only put code in the `Draw Event` that actually draws something.

Another thing to note is that the `Draw Event` will fire for every instance in your room, unless that instance has the "Visible" object property unchecked. If you add your own **Draw Event** to an object, be aware that you will override the default **Draw Event**; if you don't place code in your **Draw Event** that actually draws the object's sprite, then your instance will not show up. The easiest way to tell GameMaker to draw an object is to use the **draw_self** function like this:

**Draw Event**

```
/// We added our own draw event that will override the default
// draw event so we have to make sure to draw the object
// ourselves.
draw_self();
```

The order in which you draw the different elements in your **Draw Event** will affect how they layer in your game. Items that you draw first will show up behind any items drawn afterwards.

**Draw Event**

```
/// Draw a textbox
draw_rectangle(x-48,y-24,x+48,y+24,false);

// Draw some text. This will be drawn on top of the rectangle
var col=c_white;
draw_set_halign(fa_center);
draw_set_valign(fa_middle);
draw_text_colour(x,y,"Hello GameMaker",col,col,col,col,1);
```

We start by drawing a rectangle. Because this rectangle is drawn first, it will be below any items that we draw afterwards. The **draw_rectangle** function takes two x and y coordinate pairs. The first pair is the upper-left corner and the second pair is the lower-right corner. The last argument asks if the rectangle should be just an outline or if it should be filled. This rectangle will be drawn in black because that is the default color. After drawing the rectangle, we create a temporary variable called **col** that holds the color for the text that we will draw. We set the horizontal alignment to a center alignment using **draw_set_halign**. Then, we set the vertical alignment to a middle alignment using **draw_set_valign**. Once our setup is done, we draw the text using the **draw_text_color** function.

The first two arguments are the position of the text, the third is the text to draw, the next four are the colors to use (one for each corner of the text, as this function can be used to create a gradient in the text), and the final is the alpha value of the text.

## Draw GUI Event

The **Draw GUI Event** exists on a separate plane from the **Draw Event**, but works similarly to it. Everything drawn in the **Draw GUI Event** will be drawn on top of the items drawn in the **Draw Event**. The **Draw GUI Event** may also have a different resolution than the **Draw Event** depending on how you setup your views. I won't give any examples here on the **Draw Gui Event** because Chapter 12 has a more detailed explanation of the **Draw GUI Event** and some examples.

# Chapter 10
# Game Audio

Sounds are easiest to explain by going through a simple example. In this example, we will create a button that the user can click on. When the button is pressed, it will play a sound. This example will also be divided up into two parts. In the first part of the example, the sound won't have any effects; however, in the second part, we will use a sound emitter to alter the pitch (how high or low the sound is on the musical scale) and the gain (the loudness of the sound).

The first thing that we need to do for this example is to add a new sprite. I've named my sprite `spr_button`. It is 32 x 32 pixels in size, its origin is centered, and it is a simple black box.

● `spr_button`

Here is an image of my sprite:

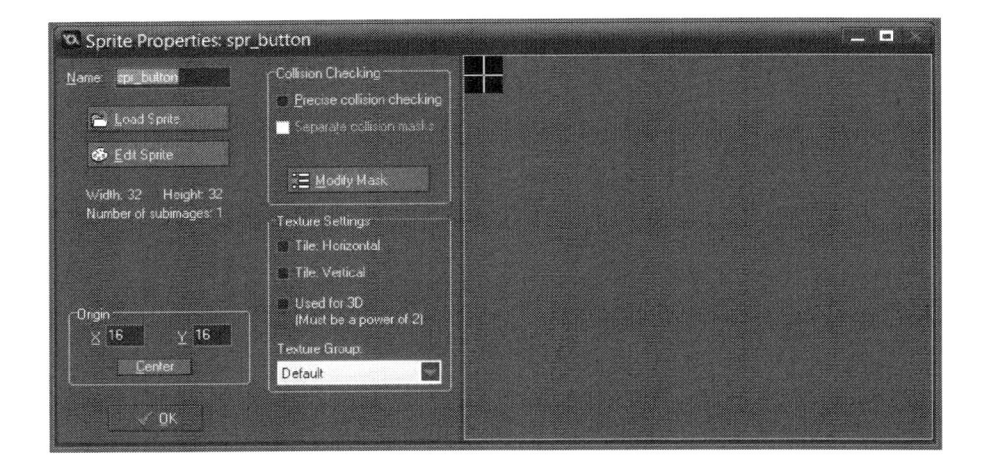

109

Once the sprite has been created, we need to create its accompanying object. I've named my object **obj_button**. For now, we won't add any events to this object. Let's first create the sound we will be using.

- `obj_button`

Add a new sound to the game. If you like, you can use _bfxr.net_ to create a sound. I've named my sound **snd_click**.

- `snd_click`

I also made the sound a "Stereo" sound using the dropdown option in the "Target Options" section of the sound properties. This gives the sound two audio channels. You could use this to play a sound only in the right speaker if the sound is coming from the right in the game or to play it only in the left speaker if the sound is coming from the left. Here is a screenshot of my sound's properties:

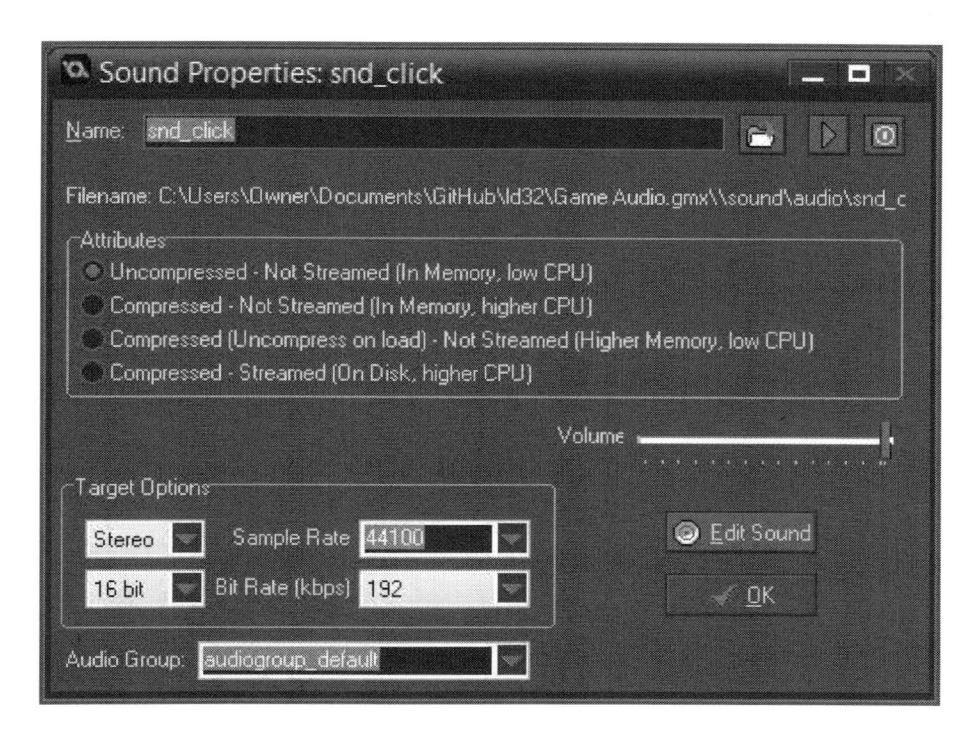

110

The sound is added and ready to go! Open up the button object and add a new **Mouse > Left Pressed Event** to it. Inside this event, we will be executing the following code.

**obj_button: Left Pressed Event**

```
/// Play the sound
audio_play_sound(snd_click,10,false);
```

This short bit of code will use the **audio_play_sound** function to play our click sound when the user clicks on the button. This function takes three arguments. This first argument is the id of the sound to play. The second argument is the priority of the sound. The priority can be from 0 to 100; it helps GameMaker decided which sounds to play if there are too many playing at the same time. Higher numbers have a higher priority. The final argument tells GameMaker whether the sound should loop or not. We don't want our sound to loop, so we pass a value of **false**.

Create a simple room, add the button object to the room, run the game, and test the project. The sound should play whenever the button is clicked.

So far, so good. Now that you know how to create a sound and play it when an event occurs, we have a problem: If you press the button multiple times in a row, the sound can get annoying. This is normal. No matter how good your sound is, if you hear it too many times in a row, it will become annoying. I'm going to teach you a trick that you can use to help mitigate this problem.

Open up the button object again, and this time, add a new **Create Event** to it.

**obj_button: Create Event**

```
/// Create a sound emitter
audio_em=audio_emitter_create();
```

In the code above, we are creating a new audio emitter and assigning its id to the **audio_em** variable.

You probably remember from the introduction to this chapter that audio emitters can be used to alter the properties of a sound that is being played. The two most common properties that are altered are the pitch and the gain. We will be altering both of these properties of our sound; this will create a nice variance and prevent the sound from becoming annoying. First though, we need to make sure to destroy the emitter when the game ends. Add a new **Game End Event** to the button object.

**obj_button: Game End Event**

```
/// Destroy the sound emitter
audio_emitter_free(audio_em);
```

In this code, we pass the **audio_em** variable into the **audio_emitter_free** function in order to destroy our audio emitter.

Now, we need to jump back to our **Mouse > Left Pressed Event** and change the way that we play our sound. Make sure that you completely remove the code that was previously in the event before adding this new code.

**obj_button: Left Pressed Event**

```
/// Play the sound
audio_emitter_pitch(audio_em,random_range(.5,1.5));
audio_emitter_gain(audio_em,random_range(.1,1));
audio_play_sound_on(audio_em,snd_click,false,10);
```

We start by calling the **audio_emitter_pitch** function. We tell it what emitter we want to use and the pitch that we want our emitter to be set to. We pass in a random range from **.5** to **1.5**. A normal pitch is set at **1**. Next, we use the **audio_emitter_gain** function. We also pass in the emitter and use a random range of **.1** to **1**. Again, the normal gain for a sound is **1**. Finally, we play the sound using the **audio_play_sound_on** function. The first argument for this function is the emitter to be used, the second is the id of the sound, the third is whether or not the sound should loop, and the fourth is the priority of the sound. It is unfortunate that the last two arguments are swapped in this function from how they are ordered in the `audio_play_sound` function, but if you know that, it makes this function easier to manage.

Run the game again and listen to the difference. I tried to use fairly drastic numbers in this example so that you will be able to hear the difference. If you still don't notice a difference, you might try changing the random ranges until you do.

Great job! Now, you know how to use sounds in GameMaker, and you even know how to alter their pitch and gain during the game to create a better audio feedback experience.

# Chapter 11
# Development Patterns and Tricks

## States

Setting up a *state system* in an object is smart if you want it to have different behaviors. Let's say you want your player object to be able to run, swing a sword, roll out of the way of enemy attacks, and then continue running. These three behaviors could have their own states within the object. There are different ways of implementing this kind of system, but I can show you some of the ways that have been helpful to me in the past.

When I was first learning to set up state systems, I tried creating a different object for each state and then I would use **instance_change** to change states. This worked, but not very well. **instance_change** is good for some things, but I wouldn't recommend it for a state system. After trying that, I realized that I could just use a state variable combined with a switch statement in the **Step Event**. Let me show you.

**Create Event**

```
/// Create the state variable
state='idle';
```

**Step Event**

```
/// Control the state
switch(state) {
        case 'idle' :
                scr_idle();
                break;
```

```
        case 'move' :
                scr_move();
                break;
        case 'attack' :
                scr_attack();
                break;
        case 'roll' :
                scr_roll();
                break;
}
```

In order to help me to organize my code better, I chose to create a script for each state and then just run the scripts for each case.

I've learned several different ways of doing this, and I discovered one that I like quite a bit. Of course, it isn't perfect either and could be improved, but it's pretty simple and easy to understand. This method uses a combination of macros and `script_execute`. Let me show you a simple example of how it works.

One of the cool features of GameMaker is that you can assign an expression to a macro. You can also assign a script to a macro. For the sake of this example, I'll use some fake code with the assignment operator but in reality, you will simply use the GameMaker user interface to create the macro.

```
PLAYER_WALK=scr_player_walk
```

Once you have this as your macro, you can set your state in the **Create Event** like this:

```
state=PLAYER_WALK;
```

You can use the same method to change the state of your object inside other events. After doing these first two steps, you still need to actually run the code associated with that state. To do so, you would place this in the **Step Event** of your object.

```
execute_script(state);
```

It's that simple! In the first step, you assign the script's id to the macro/constant. In the second step, you assign that macro/constant (which now contains the script's id) to the state variable. In the last step, you execute whatever script is assigned to the state. It's a simple method, but it can work really well for separating the code of each state.

Because enums are global in scope, you can use enums instead of macros. Either way works fine. Sometimes I find that macros are better, because you get syntax highlighting on macros, but you don't on enums.

Here is an example of how you might set up your states with an enum, instead of using macros:

```
enum state {
        walk=scr_player_walk;
}
```

You can set the state in almost the same way.

```
state=state.walk;
```

Executing the state will be done in exactly the same way. In the chapter on artificial intelligence, I go through a basic example of how you can use enums and states to create artificial intelligence for your enemies; if this section is a little confusing to you, be sure to check there for an in-game example.

## Creating Pseudo-Objects using Arrays and Enums

While developing this book, I've been working on a method for creating arrays that are similar to objects. There are many situations in which you need to store some information in an organized way and access it later, but where creating an actual object in your game would be overkill, because the built-in objects in GameMaker come with a lot of extra baggage. Of course, it is possible to use **ds_maps** for this, but maps can become bloated and difficult to manage if you try to go three levels down (for example, if you try to access a map data structure that is nested inside another map data structure). I can simulate the three-level depth using a 2d array and a few enums. Let me show you what I mean:

```
enum base {
        name=0,
        hp=1,
        att=2,
        def=3,
        spd=4
}

enum class {
        wizard=0,
        knight=1,
}
```

You can use enums to make the code more readable and avoid "magic" numbers. A magic number is a number in your code that has little obvious meaning to the person reading/writing the code. Once you have set up the enums, you can start creating the 2d arrays.

```
stats[class.wizard, base.name]="Merlin";
stats[class.wizard, base.hp]=25;
stats[class.wizard, base.att]=3;
stats[class.wizard, base.def]=1;
```

117

```
stats[class.wizard, base.spd]=3;

stats[class.knight, base.name]="Arthur";
stats[class.knight, base.hp]=35;
stats[class.knight, base.att]=5;
stats[class.knight, base.def]=2;
stats[class.knight, base.spd]=1;
```

I would recommend creating a script (where the values being passed are the arguments) to set these up. The nice thing about this method is that later in your game, you can access this data in a way that is very readable. Let me show you.

```
var damage=stats[class.wizard, base.att];
enemy.hp-=damage;
```

This example assumes that you have a reference to the "enemy" that you are attacking, but you get the idea. If you didn't use enums, it would look something like this:

```
stats[0, 1]="Merlin";
stats[0, 2]=25;
stats[0, 3]=3;
stats[0, 4]=1;
stats[0, 5]=3;
```

Do you see what I mean about magic numbers? Nobody would be able to understand this code. It would still be easy to access, but you would have to memorize the number, stat, and name associations.

## Make an Object Follow the Mouse

It's a pretty simple task to get an object to follow the mouse, but some readers might not know how to do this, so I'm going to put a quick example in. The trick with this functionality is making sure that you use the **End Step Event.**

End Step Event

```
x=mouse_x;
y=mouse_y;
```

This code sets the x position of the object to the current x position of the mouse at the end of every game step. If you use the normal **Step Event**, the timing of the move will be off, and the object will appear to lag behind the mouse.

## Make a Gun Aim Towards the Mouse.

Coding this function is also a simple task. The trick here is knowing how to use the built-in **image_angle** property and the **point_direction** function.

```
var dir=point_direction(x,y,mouse_x, mouse_y);
image_angle=dir;
direction=dir;
```

You should also make sure that your sprite has its origin where you want the pivot point to be, and that the sprite starts out facing exactly to the right (or 0 degrees).

## Using Median or Clamp

One neat trick that you can do is use the **median** function or the **clamp** function. Both of these functions can be used to limit a variable or property to a specific range. One common use for these functions is limiting the player's movement to the room.

119

`obj_player: Step Event`

```
/// Limit the player's movement
x=clamp(x,0,room_width);
y=clamp(y,0,room_height);
```

This is a simple piece of code that clamps the player's x and y coordinates to the room boundaries. Alternatively, you could do this using median.

```
x=median(0,x,room_width);
y=median(0,y,room_height);
```

You can use either method, but I feel that clamp is a more specific word and that clamp makes the code more readable.

## Colors

GameMaker has some built-in colors that you can use when drawing sprites or shapes. These colors are convenient, but I wouldn't recommend using them in most cases because they are very bland. Some of them work okay for particles, but even in this case, I generally avoid them. In the next segment, I'll show you how you can create your own custom colors, but first, let me list the built-in colors.

```
c_white
c_ltgray
c_gray
c_dkgray
c_black

c_fuchsia
c_purple

c_yellow
c_orange
```

```
c_red
c_maroon

c_lime
c_green

c_teal
c_agua
c_blue
c_navy

c_silver
c_olive
```

## Custom Colors

Making your own draw colors is important for helping your game's graphics match; you may want buttons or text to share a common color with a character or background. There are a few simple functions that you can use to more subtly adjust colors.

```
my_green=make_colour_rgb(105,205,85);
```

The `make_colour_rgb` function used in the above code takes three arguments: a red value, a green value, and a blue value (or RGB). In most graphics programs, these RGB values are displayed when you create a custom color.

```
my_red=make_colour_hsv(0,58,80);
```

The `make_colour_hsv` function also takes three arguments, a hue, a saturation, and a value. These values will also typically show up while editing colors in any graphics program. I generally use paint.net (go to getpaint.net to download a copy). Paint.net is free and quite powerful for the price.

```
my_orange=merge_colour(c_red,c_yellow,.5);
```

The `merge_colour` function takes two colors and blends them together to make a new color. The first two arguments are the colors to be used. The last argument is a number between 0 and 1 that represents the blend value for the color. A blend value of 0 will return the first color entered (`c_red`). A blend value of 1 will return the second color (`c_yellow`). A blend value of .5 will use 50% of each color.

## User Input

In GameMaker Studio, there are many different ways that you can get input from the user. In this chapter, I will be covering the three most common methods: mouse input, keyboard input, and gamepad (controller) input.

## Mouse Input

Keyboard input and mouse input are arguably the most common forms of input on computers. Mouse input in GameMaker Studio is simple and easy to learn. You can use the built-in object events, but I'm also going to show you how to check those events in code.

Let's begin by showing how to check, in code, if a mouse button is being pressed.

```
if (mouse_check_button(mb_left)) {
    // The left mouse button is being pressed
}
```

`mb_left` is a constant in GameMaker Language that refers to the left mouse button. There are constants for each of the other mouse buttons.

```
mb_none  // No mouse button
mb_left  // Left mouse button
mb_right        // Right mouse button
mb_middle       // Middle mouse button
mb_any   // Any mouse button
```

`mouse_check_button()` is a function that returns true if the button is being pressed and returns false if it is not. At this point, I should clarify the difference between the case in which the mouse button is *being* pressed and the case in which the mouse button *is (now)* pressed. The first case implies that if the user is holding the button down, it would still return true. The second implies it the function will only return true in the step in which the mouse button is (initially) pressed down. After that, it will return false, even if the user continues to hold the button down. Let's look at how you can check to see if the mouse is pressed.

```
if (mouse_check_button_pressed(mb_left)) {
        // The left mouse button was pressed.
}
```

## Mouse Position

In GameMaker Language, there are two variables that you can use to access the mouse position.

```
mouse_x
mouse_y
```

These two variables are global, and as such, can be accessed inside any object. If you wanted to make an object follow the mouse position, you could use this simple code.

### End Step Event

```
x=mouse_x;
y=mouse_y;
```

As discussed above, because of event timing issues, you will most often want to make an object follow the mouse (or another object) in the **End Step Event**.

## Keyboard Input

Keyboard input is pretty easy to learn how to use if you already know how to use mouse input, as the two are very similar.

```
if (keyboard_check(vk_right)) {
        // The right arrow key is being pressed
}
```

**vk_right** is a constant that is similar to the **mb_left** constant that the mouse input uses. There are quite a few different **vk_** prefixed constants that you can use.

```
vk_right              // Right arrow key
vk_left           // Left arrow key
vk_up             // Up arrow key
vk_down           // Down arrow key
vk_nokey              // No key
vk_anykey         // Any key
vk_enter              // Enter key
vk_escape         // Escape key
vk_space              // Space key
vk_shift          // Shift key
vk_control        // Control key
vk_alt            // Alt key
```

124

There are many more key constants than this. Most of them are rather obvious. If you want the full list, you can search for them in the GameMaker help file.

The important thing to note is that you cannot use letter keys like this:

```
if (keyboard_check(vk_a)) {
        // Causes an error
}
```

If you want to check whether the player has pressed any of the letter keys, you need to use a special function.

```
if (keyboard_check(ord('A'))) {
        // The "A" key is being pressed
}
```

Maybe you want to check for any key and then display the key pressed to the screen. You can do that like this:

```
if (keyboard_check(vk_any)) {
        show_message(keyboard_lastchar);
}
```

**keyboard_lastchar** will return a string of the last keyboard key pressed. This will only work with letters and numbers though; it returns an empty string for any other keys. If you want to check for a key that isn't a number or a letter you can use **keyboard_key**. This global variable returns the ASCII value of the key pressed.

```
if (keyboard_check(vk_any)) {
        show_message(string(keyboard_key));
}
```

125

There will be times when you want to have two keys do the same exact thing. For example, many games allow the player to use either the arrow keys or the WASD letter keys to move the character. You can map keys to each other like this.

```
// Map the ASDW keys to the arrow keys
keyboard_set_map(ord('D'), vk_right);
keyboard_set_map(ord('A'), vk_left);
keyboard_set_map(ord('W'), vk_up);
keyboard_set_map(ord('S'), vk_down);
```

You only need to call these functions once, for example, in a character object's **Create Event**. You would continue to program your game and character using the arrow keys, but the WASD keys would work as well, because they are mapped to the arrow keys.

## GamePad Input

Using gamepad input is a little harder than keyboard input, but it is very similar. Most of the time, you will want your game to be compatible with several input devices. You may have it set up so that the player can use the keyboard (by default), but if they plug in a gamepad, then the keyboard will be disabled and the gamepad will be used for control. Let me show you a simple example that allows you to do this.

```
var device=0;
if (gamepad_is_connected(device)) {
        // Get gamepad input
} else {
        // Get keyboard input
}
```

This code checks to see whether the first ($0^{th}$) gamepad is connected. The device number is the assigned player number. If your controller's light indicates that you are player number one, then the device number should be 0. If it shows that you are player number two, then the device number should be 1. The device number is important, because it is used in most

126

functions for getting gamepad input; let's look at some of them. Assume that the device number is still 0.

```
if(gamepad_button_check(device, gp_face1)) {
        // Do something cool
}
```

This function checks to see whether the user is pressing a button on the gamepad. The button being checked is **gp_face1**; on an Xbox controller, this is the "A" button. There is an entire list of button constants that can be used with these functions. You can check the GameMaker help file for the list of controller constants.

## Methods of Controlling Input

The method that I generally use for controlling input is to separate the input from the actual movement with variables. This allows me to move a character or enemy with the variables created. I'm going to set up a simple example of this.

First let's create the variables.

**Create Event**

```
xaxis=0;
yaxis=0;
abtn=false;
```

Now let's set them in our player, based on the input.

**Step Event**

```
if (gamepad_is_connected(0)) {
        // Get gamepad input
        xaxis=gamepad_axis_value(0,gp_axislh);
        yaxis=gamepad_axis_value(0,gp_axislv);
        abtn=gamepad_button_check(0,gp_face1);

} else {
```

127

```
        // Get keyboard input
        var right=keyboard_check(vk_right);
        var left=keyboard_check(vk_left);
        var up=keyboard_check(vk_up);
        var down=keyboard_check(vk_down);

        xaxis=right-left;
        yaxis=down-up;
        abtn=keyboard_check(ord('A'));
}
```

Once you have created the variables and set them according to the input the player has given us, you can decide how to move the player. This code assumes that you are using **obj_solid** as your walls.

### Step Event

```
// Set the speed
var spd=4;

// Horizontal movement
if (!place_meeting(x+xaxis*spd,y,obj_solid)) {
        x+=xaxis*spd;
}

// Vertical movement
if (!place_meeting(x,y+yaxis*spd,obj_solid)) {
        y+=yaxis*spd;
}

if (abtn) {
        // Shoot a bullet
        instance_create(x,y,obj_bullet);
}
```

As you can see, it is easy to separate the input from the control of the object, which allows us to pass any input type into this object and still have the same player behavior.

Chapter 12

# Drawing on the GUI Layer

## Draw GUI Event

GUI stands for graphical user interface. The **Draw GUI Event** is different from the **Draw Event** because the **Draw GUI Event** draws everything relative to the *GUI layer* and not relative to the actual game room. Often, the GUI layer seems to be relative to the view, and most of the time it is, but be aware that this isn't always true.

Often, when people start using the **Draw GUI Event** in conjunction with views, they run into scaling issues. There is a handly little function that you can use to resolve this.

```
display_set_gui_size(640,360);
```

`display_set_gui_size` takes a width and a height. You want to make sure that the width and the height of the GUI are the same as the width and height of your view so that the GUI surface will have the same resolution as the view. By default, the GUI layer seems to be the same resolution as the port on the screen.

Here is a good way to set the GUI's display size to the size of the view, no matter what the actual size of the view is. Place this code in the **Create Event** of your object:

```
/// Set the GUI to the size of the view
```

```
var view_width=view_wview[view_current];
var view_height=view_hview[view_current];
display_set_gui_size(view_width,view_height);
```

Once you have the correct height and width, the **Draw GUI Event** is used just like the **Draw Event**. The output is different, but you can still use all the normal draw functions in this event. Let's quickly draw some text using the **Draw GUI Event**.

```
draw_text(32,32,"Hello Draw GUI!");
```

This simple code will draw the text "Hello Draw GUI" at position (32,32) of the view. It won't matter if the player moves inside the room, the text will still be drawn relative to the view. As you can see, the **draw_text** function is used exactly like it would be in a normal **Draw Event**, but it works differently. You will also notice that the text is on top of the other objects in the room, regardless of the depth of the object that actually draws it. This is because the GUI layer is, by default, drawn on top of the rest of the room.

As you are drawing on the GUI layer, you may need to get information about the GUI layer. Here are some functions that you can use to get this information:

```
var gui_width=display_get_gui_width();
var gui_height=display_get_gui_height();
draw_text(gui_width-32,gui_height-32,"Hello Draw GUI!");
```

This code does the same thing as the code above it, but it draws the text at the lower right-hand corner of the display. We get references to the width and height of the GUI layer in order to draw our text relative to those dimensions.

## Creating Buttons on the GUI Layer

One of the most difficult things to deal with on the GUI layer is drawing buttons. This is because the GUI layer is independent of the application surface. The calculations for determining if the mouse is hovering over a button can be tricky. Let me show you how I have solved this problem with an example.

Create a new sprite and name it `spr_player`.

- `spr_player`

I've made my sprite a black 32 x 32 square. Now create two new objects. Name one of them `obj_player` and the other one `obj_gui_button`.

- `obj_player`
- `obj_gui_button`

Create a new room and name it `rm_test`. Give the room a width of 640 and a height of 360. Click on the views tab, click "Enable the use of Views", click "Visible when room starts", set the view width and height to 320 x 180, and set the port width and height to 640 x 360. Set the "Object following" to `obj_player`, the horizontal border (Hbor) to 160 and the vertical border (Vbor) to 90. This will force the view to follow our player object. Now, place both the player object and the GUI button in the room. Make sure that the GUI button falls inside the view. We are going to use its starting position to determine its position on the GUI Layer. Here is a screenshot of the room and its view properties.

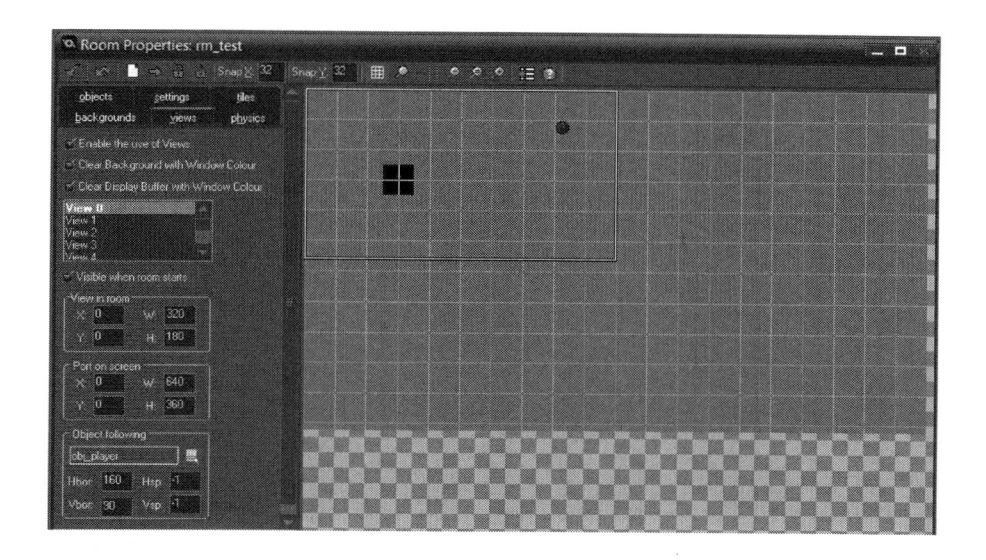

You can see that I have also placed a basic green background in my room. It isn't necessary, but you can add a background as well, if you want.

Open up the player object and add a **Step Event** to it. This event will hold the code that moves the player in the room. We need the player object to move so that we can make sure that the GUI button object follows the view correctly. Here is the code that will go in the **Step Event**.

**obj_player: Step Event**

```
// Move the player
var spd=4;
var up=keyboard_check(vk_up);
var down=keyboard_check(vk_down);
var left=keyboard_check(vk_left);
var right=keyboard_check(vk_right);

x+=(right-left)*spd;
y+=(down-up)*spd;
```

This is some shortcut code that moves the player using the arrow keys.

Now, open up the GUI button object and add a new **Create Event**. Drag over a **Code Action** and place this code block in it.

132

### obj_gui_button: Create Event

```
/// Initialize the GUI button
text='Click Me';
width=96;
height=28;
hover=false;
scale=2;

// This is the button object's position relative to the GUI
layer.
display_x=xstart*scale;
display_y=ystart*scale;
```

We start by creating some instance variables that will define how our button looks and behaves. The **text** variable holds a string value of the text that will be shown on the button. After that, we have the **width** and **height**. Then we have a variable called **hover**. Our **hover** variable will be true if the mouse is over the button and false if it is not. We also create a variable called **scale** and set it to 2. Our scale is set to 2 because the GUI layer defaults to the size of the port on the screen and the port on the screen is *twice* the size of the view. After creating the initial instance variables, we create two new instance variables that will be used to position the button on the GUI layer. These two variables will grab the button object's starting position in the room and multiply it by our **scale**.

Add a new **End Step Event**. In this event, we will do the math necessary to calculate whether the mouse is hovering over our button.

### obj_gui_button: End Step Event

```
/// Check to see if the mouse is above the button
// Find the edges
var leftx=display_x-width/scale;
var rightx=display_x+width/scale;
var topy=display_y-height/scale;
var bottomy=display_y+height/scale;

// Get the window position of the mouse
var wmx=window_mouse_get_x();
var wmy=window_mouse_get_y();
```

```
// Check to see if the mouse is inside the edges
hover=point_in_rectangle(wmx,wmy,leftx,topy,rightx,bottomy);
```

First, we get the edges of the button. Next, we get the mouse's window position. If the view has moved, the window position of the mouse will be different from the mouse's position in the room. Lastly, we use the **point_in_rectangle** function to determine whether the mouse is hovering over the GUI button. The **point_in_rectangle** function takes six arguments. The first two are the point to check, the next two are the upper-left corner of the rectangle, and the final two are the lower-right corner of the rectangle.

Add a **Mouse > Global Mouse > Global Left Pressed Event** to the GUI button object. Drag over a **Code Action** and type this code in it.

**obj_gui_button: Global Left Pressed Event**

```
/// Click the button
if (hover) {
        show_message("You clicked the button.");
}
```

This code checks to make sure that we are over the button when the mouse button is pressed. If we are, it shows a message saying that the button was clicked. We can't use the **Left Pressed Event** because this button object doesn't have a collision box. Even if it did, we are working on the GUI layer, and the collision box would be in a different location from the drawn button.

The last event that we need to add to our GUI button object is the event that will draw the button on the screen. We are using the **Draw GUI Event**.

134

### obj_gui_button: Draw GUI Event

```
/// Draw the GUI button
if (hover) {
        draw_set_alpha(.2);
} else {
        draw_set_alpha(.5);
}

var leftx=display_x-width/scale;
var topy=display_y-height/scale;
var rightx=display_x+width/scale;
var bottomy=display_y+height/scale;

// Draw the button using a rectangle
draw_rectangle(leftx,topy,rightx,bottomy,false);
draw_set_alpha(1);

// Set the horizontal and vertical alignments for text
draw_set_halign(fa_center);
draw_set_valign(fa_middle);

// Draw the button text
var col=c_white;
draw_text_colour(display_x,display_y,text,col,col,col,col,1);
```

Using the **hover** variable that we created earlier, we set the draw alpha to either 0.2 or 0.5. This makes it easier to see the button if the mouse is hovering over it. We create some temporary variables to help us find the corners of the button and use the **draw_rectangle** function to draw our button. After drawing the button, we make sure to set the draw alpha back to 1. We set the text alignment to center and middle, and then, we draw the text over the button.

## Testing the Game
Run the game and make sure that, no matter where the player is in the room, the button responds to being hovered over and clicked on.

Working with the GUI layer can be a little tricky sometimes, but often, it is well worth the work. Keep in mind, you don't always need to use the GUI layer for HUDs, menus, and buttons. Sometimes you can make it work just by drawing relative to the view. Personally, I do whatever is going to take the least amount of code and still look good. For game start menus, I use normal objects, but for HUD items that don't need any interaction (like health and lives), I will use the GUI layer because I don't need to calculate the position using the view. Mess around with the previous examples and find out what works best for you.

# Chapter 13
# Particles and Surfaces

## Creating particle systems
A *particle system* is a world that the particles live in. In GameMaker, it is impossible to create particles without first creating a particle system. Creating a particle system is actually easier than creating the particles themselves. Think of it this way. For objects, you must first create a room to put them in or the objects can't be used or seen. Particle systems are like the room and the particles are like the objects. In most cases, you will only need to create one particle system to contain all of your particles. Because there is generally only one, I like to create an object for controlling the particles and the particle system. In this object, I create a global variable and assign the particle system to it like this. I would place this code in the `Game Start Event` of an object created specifically to manage the particles.

```
global.ps=part_system_create();
```

After creating the particle system and assigning it to a global variable, you can reference it at any time. You are now ready to create your first particle type.

## Creating particle types
The particle is going to be used by multiple objects, so I'm going to make it global, just like the particle system. This function just creates the particle type. Remember, though, this function does not actually create particles, it just defines the particle type! Later, you will use this particle type to actually create some particles inside of your particle system, which will display them in the room.

```
global.pt_blood=part_type_create();
```

Now that you have created the particle type, you need to set the different properties. The properties that you set will determine the look and behavior of this particle type. There are lots of different properties to set. I will explain each one as it gets set.

I also like to create a local reference to the particle type for easier access while setting properties.

```
var pt=global.pt_blood;
```

The last line allows us to use **pt** as the id for the particle type, which is less typing. Let's set the shape of the particle.

```
part_type_shape(pt,pt_shape_disk);
```

The first argument is the id of the particle type. I use **pt**, which is a reference to the particle type already created. The second argument is the particle shape. There are quite a few different built-in shapes. Here is a quick reference list of them:

**Particle Shape Types**

    pt_shape_disk
    pt_shape_pixel
    pt_shape_line
    pt_shape_star
    pt_shape_sphere
    pt_shape_flare
    pt_shape_spark
    pt_shape_explosion
    pt_shape_snow

```
pt_shape_smoke
pt_shape_cloud
pt_shape_square
pt_shape_circle
pt_shape_ring
```

Try them all out to see what they look like, and find the ones that will best suit your style! You may have to adjust the sizes and colors to get a good idea of what they look like. I'll show you how to do that now.

```
part_type_size(pt,0.1,0.2,0,0);
```

This bit of code sets the size. There are five arguments: the first is the id, the second is the minimum size, the third is the maximum size, the fourth is the size increase, and the fifth is the size wiggle. I'm not going to explain exactly what each argument does. If you want to know more about that, you can check out the GameMaker help file or just mess around with the values.

```
part_type_type_color2(pt,c_red,c_maroon);
```

This bit of code will change the particle from red to maroon along the span of its life. Let's set the particle speed now.

```
part_type_speed(pt,2,5,-0.1,0);
```

The first argument is obviously the id again. After that, it is the minimum speed of the particle, the maximum speed, the amount to add to the speed at each step (you will notice that I am actually subtracting from the speed each step), and finally the amount to wiggle.

```
part_type_direction(pt,0,360,0,0);
```

This function sets the direction in which the particle will travel. Once again, you notice that the first argument is the id. After the id, there is a minimum direction, a maximum direction, a direction increase, and a direction wiggle. You may be noticing a pattern with these functions. For the most part, they are all very similar.

```
part_type_gravity(pt,0.2,270);
```

Now let's set how gravity influences these particles. After the id argument at the start, there is a gravity amount argument followed by a gravity direction argument. As you probably know by now, 270 degrees is the downward direction.

You are finished creating the particle type and setting all of the different attributes of your new particle type. Now it's almost time to actually create some particles. Before you move on, you need to make sure to destroy the particle system and particle types in the **Game End Event** so that you don't create a memory leak. It is pretty easy to do.

**Game End Event**

```
part_type_destroy(global.pt_blood);
part_system_destroy(global.ps);
```

And you're done!

## Creating particles

This part is where it gets fun. Let's create some actual particles. First, I'm going to show you how to create particles without using an emitter. You might not know what a particle emitter is, and that's okay. I will explain it after this. If you are just testing your particles, you can place this next bit of code in a **Global Mouse, Left Pressed Event**.

### Global Mouse, Left Pressed Event

```
var mx=mouse_x;
var my=mouse_y;
part_particles_create(global.ps,mx,my,global.pt_blood,10);
```

This code will create ten blood particles at the mouse's position. The first argument is the system that you want to create the particles in; the second and third are the x and y positions of the particles, respectively; the fourth is the particle type that you want to use; and the last argument is the number of particles that you want to create.

## Creating particle emitters

Using `part_particles_create` is a good way for beginners to get some practice using particles, but generally, you will want to use an emitter to create your particles. Emitters are special little objects that let you create particles in bursts, in streams, across large areas of the room, and in different defined areas. The first thing you need to do in order to use an emitter is create one.

```
em=part_emitter_create(global.ps);
```

The only argument for this function is the id of the particle system that you want this emitter to live in. I generally create emitters using an instance variable (instance scope), because only the object that creates the emitter is going to use it. Placing it in the global scope would generally be pointless.

After creating the emitter, you need to set the region that the emitter will create particles in. This is a simple function that looks like this:

```
var mx=mouse_x;
var my=mouse_y;
var shape=ps_shape_ellipse;
var disr=ps_distr_gaussian;
```

141

```
part_emitter_region(global.ps,em,mx-4,mx+4,my-4,my+4,shape,disr);
```

There are a few strange things that you might notice about the arguments passed into this function. Let's go over them. The first argument is the particle system id. After that, we have the emitter id, the x minimum, the x maximum, the y minimum, the y maximum, the emitter shape, and the particle distribution type.

The *emitter shape* is a global constant defined by GameMaker. Here is a list of the different emitter shapes that you can use:

**Particle Distribution Shape Types**

```
pt_shape_rectangle
pt_shape_ellipse
pt_shape_diamond
pt_shape_line
```

The *particle distribution type* is also a global constant defined by GameMaker. There are only three different types that you can use. Here they are:

**Particle Distribution Types**

```
ps_distr_linear
ps_distr_gaussian
ps_distr_invgaussian
```

The *linear distribution* is an even distribution across the region of the emitter. The *gaussian distribution* creates more particles near the center of the shape and fewer particles closer to the outside of the shape. The *invgaussian* is an inverse of the gaussian, creating more particles near the edges.

## Creating Particles Using an Emitter

Now that the emitter is all set up, you are ready to create some particles using it. There are a few different functions that you can use now with your emitter. I'll show each one to you and teach you what they do.

```
part_emitter_stream(global.ps,em,global.pt_blood,2);
```

Once again, the arguments start with the particle system id. Then, you have the emitter id, the particle type, and the number of particles to create. The function will create a stream of particles. Every step, it will create two blood particles. This function can be placed in the **Create Event** of an object and will continue to stream particles even after the **Create Event** has ended. If you want to stop the stream of particles, you will need to call this function again and set the number of particles created to zero.

Streaming is cool for water fountains, snow, rain, and such. For blood, on the other hand, our character would be constantly bleeding out. Here is how you can create a burst of blood particles:

```
part_emitter_burst(global.ps,em,global.pt_blood,10);
```

The arguments are all exactly the same as those for the streaming function. The difference is that this is a one-time call that will stop creating particles once it has been run. I generally like bursting more often than streaming, but you can mess around with both of them.

Great job! You have now learned to create a particle system, particle types to live in the system, and emitters to create those particle types. The best way to learn more about particles is to create a simple particle game and mess around with the different values for your particle emitters and particle types until you get something you like. It can be a great way to come up with new particle types, and you will have loads of fun while doing it.

## Surfaces

If you have ever used GameMaker, you have already used a *surface*. Sprites associated with objects are draw on what is called the application surface. This is the room/view combination that comes up when we run our game. It is even possible to manipulate the application surface, but for now, we won't do that. The only difference between the application surface and another surface that we might create is that the application surface is drawn on the screen automatically and your surface isn't. In fact, if we don't draw our surface manually, we will never be able to see it. Once we have created our surface and drawn something to it, we need to actually draw the surface itself (or pieces of it) onto the application surface so that the person playing your game will see it.

Surfaces are an amazing feature of GameMaker Language, but if not used correctly, they are also a little volatile (even unstable). There is only one surface that isn't volatile—the application surface. The application surface is the surface that normal draw events draw to. There are built-in functions that we can use to work around the volatility of surfaces. Using these functions, we can create our own surfaces and manipulate them. Surfaces can be used for lots of different things, but they are most commonly used for lighting effects and shadows.

Creating a surface is very easy and can be done with this simple function. The two arguments are the width and height of the surface.

**Create Event**

```
my_surface=surface_create(640,360);
```

Because they are volatile, surfaces can be removed from memory at any time. This means that there is no guarantee that the surface will still exist the next time that we try to access it. For this reason, GameMaker Language provides a function to check for the existence of a surface before it tries to do anything with it.

**Draw Event**

```
if (surface_exists(my_surface)) {
        // Work with surface
} else {
        // Create the surface again
        my_surface=surface_create(640,360);
}
```

First, we check to make sure that the surface exists. If it does, we can use it. If not, we will need to create the surface again.

Once we know that the surface is there, we can start drawing to it. To do so, we need to tell GameMaker that we want to draw on *our* surface and not to the application surface.

**Draw Event**

```
if (surface_exists(my_surface)) {
        // Tell GameMaker to draw on your surface
        surface_set_target(my_surface);

        // Now we can draw on the surface
        draw_circle_colour(32,32,16,c_red,c_red,false);

        // Tell GameMaker to reset to the application surface
        surface_reset_target();

        // Make sure to draw the new surface in the room
        draw_surface(my_surface,0,0);

}
```

After we have drawn to our surface, we will want to actually draw the surface in the room. Remember, surfaces are hidden until we actually show them to the player. We can do this using the **draw_surface** function. This function takes a surface as its first argument, with x and y coordinates as the second and third arguments, respectively.

145

Now, we will want to modify the way that we create the surface. The surface should start as a clean slate. We can do this by drawing a black background across the entire surface.

**Draw Event**

```
// Create the surface again
my_surface=surface_create(640,360);

// Tell GameMaker to draw on your surface
surface_set_target(my_surface);

// Now we can draw on the surface
draw_clear_alpha(c_black,0);

// Tell GameMaker to reset to the application surface
surface_reset_target();
```

Great job! Those are the basics of using a surface. There is one last thing about surfaces that we need to discuss: A surface must be destroyed at the end of the game to avoid memory leaks. This is the function we can call to do that:

**Game End Event**

```
if (surface_exists(my_surface)) {
        surface_free(my_surface);
}
```

## Surfaces Example Game

For our very first use of surfaces, I'm going to show you how to create a basic drawing game. This is a simple way to deal with surfaces, and it will help you get your hands dirty in some code without overcomplicating things. You won't need any sprites or backgrounds to create the simple game—just one room and one object. Let's get started!

Create a new object and name it **obj_paper**. This will be the object we use to control everything in our game. Add a **Create Event** to the object and

146

drag over a **Code Action**. When the new code window comes up, write this:

### Create Event

```
surface=noone;
mouse_xprevious=mouse_x;
mouse_yprevious=mouse_y;
```

It should be easy to recognize what this code does. We are creating three new variables. Surface is set to **noone** (because we haven't created the surface yet) and the mouse's previous two variables are set the mouse's current position. We will use these for drawing our lines later.

Now that the **Create Event** is finished, add a **Draw Event** and drag over a new, empty **Code Action**. This is going to be the most complicated section, but I'll explain it all.

### Draw Event

```
// Local variables to shorten code
var mx=mouse_x;
var my=mouse_y;
var mxp=mouse_xprevious;
var myp=mouse_yprevious;

if (surface_exists(surface)) {
        if (mouse_check_button(mb_left)) {
                surface_set_target(surface);
                draw_circle(mx,my,3,false);
                draw_line_width(mxp,myp,mx,my,8);
                surface_reset_target();
        }
        draw_surface(surface,0,0);
        mouse_xprevious=mouse_x;
        mouse_yprevious=mouse_y;
} else {
        // We need to create it
        surface=surface_create(640,360);
        surface_set_target(surface);
```

147

```
        draw_clear_alpha(c_white,1);
        surface_reset_target();
}
```

First, we check to see if the surface exists. Remember, we do this because they are volatile (it might not exist). If it doesn't exist, then we create it and draw a solid white color to the entire surface. If it does exist, we check to see if the mouse button is being pressed. If the mouse button *is* being pressed, we draw a circle at the current mouse position and a line from the last mouse position to the current mouse position.

After all that is done, we call **draw_surface** to actually draw the surface in the room (on the application surface) and update the mouse's previous positions. There are three arguments that **draw_surface** needs. The first is the id of the surface, and the other two are the x and y positions, respectively, where the surface will be drawn. That wasn't too bad, was it?

Lastly, we will need to destroy the surface when the game ends. Add a new **Game End Event** and place this code into it:

**Game End Event**

```
if (surface_exists(surface)) {
        surface_free(surface);
}
```

The game is now ready for testing! Create a room, put an instance of **obj_paper** in the room, and run the game. We should have a white paper that we can draw on using the mouse. If the room is larger than the surface size of 640 by 360, the surface doesn't take up the entire room, and there is a gray area where we can't draw. If you want, you can change your room size to match the surface size, but it is good for you to see that we are drawing the surface at position (0, 0) and that it doesn't take up the whole screen.

# Chapter 14
# Physics

## Using Physics in your Game
There are cases in which you will not want to use GameMaker's built-in physics system. You shouldn't assume that because the physics system can be really cool and fun that you should use it in your game. As a general rule, you probably won't want to add a physics system to your game unless it will add to the gameplay in some fundamental way. That being said, using physics is a great way for even new GameMaker users to create lifelike and amazing worlds. Let's get started.

## Making a Physics World
The first things that we need to do to use the physics system is create a room, click the physics tab in the room properties, and check the little box that says "Room is Physics World." If we forget to check this box, our physics system will not work.

We should also notice three other input fields underneath the checkbox. What are those? The first is the "Gravity X" value. This can be set to create horizontal gravity in our room. A positive value would be gravity to the right and a negative value would be gravity to the left. The next is the "Gravity Y" value. This can be set to create vertical gravity in our room. A positive value would be gravity in the downwards direction and a negative value would be in the upwards direction. I usually set my gravity to about 60 in the "Gravity Y" value. The last input field allows us to change the "Pixels to Meters" conversion rate. I personally leave that alone.

## Physics Object Types
In the physics system, there are three main types of objects that we will be creating: static objects, dynamic objects, and kinematic objects. Here is a short description of each type:

## Static Objects

Static objects will make up the walls of our physics game. These objects are solid and cannot be moved by collisions with other objects. They will also be unaffected by gravity.

## Dynamic Objects

Dynamic objects will likely be the most common in our game. These are normal physics objects that can be pushed, pulled, and rotated based on forces. If we have a player object, it should probably be a dynamic object.

## Kinematic Objects

Kinematic objects are like static objects, only we can move them around in the world using their x and y coordinates. An example of a kinematic object would be a moving platform or elevator.

## Making Our First Physics Object

Now that our first physics world is ready, it's time to create our physics object. This is actually easier than you might think. Quickly create a square sprite and center its origin. After doing that, create a new object and assign the square sprite to it. In the object's properties, right under the "Solid" checkbox, there is a "Uses Physics" checkbox; check that box. An additional properties window will show up. I'm going to explain each additional property in detail.

## Collision Shape

The *collision shape* of the object is a collection of points and edges that make up the collision detection boundary for the object. There are three types of shapes that we can set it to: *Circle*, *Box*, and *Shape*. Circle and Box are self explanatory. Shape isn't too complicated: we can draw our own collision shape. This is very powerful and easy to do. Just click the button that says "Modify Collision Shape" to start creating a custom shape. We may want to click the "Modify Collision Shape" button even for the Circle and Box shapes; GameMaker tries to be smart when creating them, but it often seems to get them wrong. If it does get them wrong and we don't check the shape ourselves, we may get strange collision errors.

## Density

Now, let's talk about the second property, the *density* of the object. This value is used to calculate the mass of the object, which is used by the physics system for momentum calculations. A larger value here will make our object heavier. When we set that value to zero, it gives the object an infinite density (which is how the system creates static objects).

## Restitution

*Restitution* is the third property we can set. This value is a little harder to explain... It represents how bouncy our physics object is.

## Collision Group

As our fourth property, we have *collision groups*. Collision groups can be used to prevent certain physics objects from colliding with other physics objects.

## Linear Damping

Now for property number five. The physics engine in GameMaker is attempting to simulate the real world; the *linear damping* value helps achieve this. In the real world, objects in the air experience air resistance, and this slows them down (for example, while in flight). In GameMaker's physics engine, there is no air resistance. This value simulates air resistance. If we were to set this value to zero, the object would behave as if it were moving around in a vacuum.

## Angular Damping

Our sixth property, *angular damping*, works like linear damping, only it operates on the rotation of an object. If we set this to zero and the object starts rotating and never interacts with another object, it will rotate forever. If we give this property a value, the rotation of the object will slow down over time. Generally, we will want to have some value here, because in the real world, air resistance would slow the spinning of an object.

## Friction

Lastly, we have *friction*. This one is pretty obvious. This value controls the friction that is subtracted from an object's motion when it is touching another object.

# Force vs Torque

In GameMaker's physics, there are a few different ways that we can move an object in the room. Two common ways are to apply a *force* or a *torque* to it. It is important to understand the difference between these two methods. Imagine that we build a car in our game room. We could apply a force to the car to move it, or we could apply a torque to the tires to move it. What is the difference? Well, applying a force to the car is like pushing on the car from behind. The car will start to roll and we might even be able to move the car really fast if we apply enough force, but we will never be able to spin out our tires. The better (and more realistic) method is to apply a torque to the tires. This spins the tires and moves the car forward. If we have enough torque to overcome the friction that we have set, then we will even be able to spin our tires out and burn some rubber!

# Building a Simple Car Game Using Physics

I'm really excited to teach you how to build a simple car using GameMaker's physics engine. For this first example, we will avoid modelling the suspension because that will complicate things. We will add some random terrain generation to make things more interesting.

For this example, we will need two sprites, four objects, and one room.

# Create the Sprites

For the first sprite, create a new 80 × 24 image and then fill the entire image. After creating the rectangle sprite name it **spr_car_body** and click the "center" button to center the origin. For the second sprite, create a new 40 × 40 image and draw a solid circle using the circle tool. Start at the top left corner and finish at the bottom right corner. This will create a perfect circle that uses as much of the image as possible. Name this sprite **spr_car_tire** and click the "center" button to center its origin.

# Create the Objects

The first object to create is the **obj_collision_parent** object. This object allows us to have collision be inherited uniformly across our objects (we don't have to add a **Collision Event** to all of the objects in our game). This object doesn't need a sprite. Add a new **Collision Event** to the object and have it collide with itself (**obj_collision_parent**). We technically don't need any code in this event because the physics engine will handle all of the complicated behavior. We do have to put an action in here, though, or GameMaker will delete the event. Drag over a **Code Action** and put this comment in it.

```
/// Detect the collision
```

This comment just keeps GameMaker from deleting our collision object parent.

Now, we can create the car body object. Click the "add new object" button and name the new object **obj_car_body**. Set the sprite to **spr_car_body**, give the object a parent of **obj_collision_parent**, and click the "Uses Physics" checkbox in the object's properties. Now, we can set the collision shape to "Box" and modify the collision shape to make sure that it lines up with the assigned sprite. Once we have done that, use these values for the physics properties.

**Physics Properties**

```
Density: 0.5
Restitution: 0.1
Collision Group: 0
Linear Damping: 0.1
Angular Damping: 0.1
Friction: 0.2
```

Once we have finished setting up the object properties and the physics properties, we are ready to start adding some code to this object. Add a new **Step Event** and place this code in it.

**obj_car_body: Step Event**

```
/// Force the view to follow the car
view_xview[0]=x-view_wview[0]/2;
view_yview[0]=y-view_hview[0]/2;
```

153

This code will force the view that we create in the room to follow the car body, even if the car body actually leaves the room. We will add more code to the car body in a minute, but for now, let's move on to the car tire object.

Create a new object and name it **obj_car_tire**. Set its sprite to **spr_car_tire**, give it a parent of **obj_collision_parent**, and check the "Uses Physics" checkbox in the object properties. Now, we have access to the physics properties. Set the collision shape to "Circle", modify the collision shape to make sure that it matches the sprite, and then, set the different physics properties using these values.

**Physics Properties**

```
Density: 0.5
Restitution: 0.1
Collision Group: 0
Linear Damping: 0.1
Angular Damping: 0.1
Friction: 30
```

Make sure to get the friction right. If the friction is super low, our tires will spin out on the terrain and won't be able to get any traction. Our physics properties are ready now, and it's time to add a **Create Event**. Place this code in the **Create Event** for our tire object.

**obj_car_tire: Create Event**

```
/// Initialize the tire
spd=1000;
```

This just creates a speed variable that we can use later when moving the tires. Notice, I didn't call the variable **speed**. This is because **speed** is reserved by GameMaker and should not be used with the physics system.

Now, it's time to actually add the movement code to the tires. As we discussed just a few paragraphs ago, we need to decide if we want to use a force or a torque. If we use a force, it would simulate someone pushing

154

the car from behind. If we use a torque, it would simulate an engine spinning the tires. We want to use a torque. Add a new **Keyboard Right Key Event** to our tire object and add this code:

#### obj_car_tire: Keyboard Right Key Event

```
/// Add a clockwise torque to the wheel
physics_apply_torque(spd);
```

Now, create a new **Keyboard Left Event** and add this code to it.

#### obj_car_tire: Keyboard Left Key Event

```
/// Add a counter-clockwise torque to the wheel
physics_apply_torque(-spd);
```

The tire will now spin when we press left or right! One of the things that I love about GameMaker's physics system is how it simplifies the code so much. We just set the rules for the world and the physics engine handles the rest. Our tires are now finished, and we can go back to the car body object. Open it up and add a **Create Event**. In the **Create Event**, add this code:

#### obj_car_body: Create Event

```
/// Initialize the car
var half=sprite_width/2;

var tire=instance_create(x-half+12,y,obj_car_tire);
var tx=tire.x;
var ty=tire.y;
physics_joint_revolute_create(id,tire,tx,ty,0,0,0,0,0,0,0);

var tire=instance_create(x+half-12,y,obj_car_tire);
var tx=tire.x;
var ty=tire.y;
physics_joint_revolute_create(id,tire,tx,ty,0,0,0,0,0,0,0);
```

In this code, we sometimes use half the width of our car body sprite. This number will help us to place the tire correctly. After doing that, we create the first tire and attach it using the `physics_joint_revolute_create` function. The second tire is created and attached in the same way, but we pass different `tire.x` and `tire.y` values.

The `physics_joint_revolute_create` function is one that we haven't discussed before. This function attaches physics objects or (fixtures) to each other with a rotatable joint. The first argument that we pass is the id of the car body. The next is the id of the car tire. Because we stored the id of the tire instance in the local tire variable, we can use that. Then, we pass the x and y positions of the origin of the joint. We are using the x and y positions of the tire because we already created them right where we want the joint to be. After that, there are a ton of zeros. These different arguments have to do with limiting the rotation of the joint or adding a motor speed to the joint. The last one is whether or not we want the tire to collide with the car body. We set this to 0 (or false) because we do not want them to collide. They will be touching, so a collision would mess up our car.

Once we have added this **Create Event**, our car is ready for the physics world! The only problem is that our world doesn't have any ground to drive on. It's time to create the ground object that will generate our world. We are also going to have this ground object draw the physics world with a neat function called `physics_world_draw_debug`. We probably wouldn't want to use this function for an actual game, but it will work well in this case, and we can use it to better understand how different physics objects work.

Create a new object and name it **obj_ground**. Give the new ground object a parent of **obj_collision parent**. We don't need to check "Uses Physics" for this object, because we will be doing that with code this time. Add a **Create Event** and place this code in it.

**obj_ground: Create Event**

```
/// Initialize the ground
flags=phy_debug_render_shapes |
      phy_debug_render_joints |
```

```
            phy_debug_render_coms |
            phy_debug_render_obb;

var xx=-100;
var yy=0;

var fix=physics_fixture_create();
physics_fixture_set_chain_shape(fix,false);
repeat(100) {
            physics_fixture_add_point(fix,xx,yy);
            xx+=50+random(150);
            yy+=-32+irandom(64);
            yy=median(64,yy,room_height-64);
}

physics_fixture_set_density(fix,0);
physics_fixture_set_restitution(fix,0.5);
physics_fixture_bind(fix,id);
physics_fixture_delete(fix);
```

At first glance, this code can look daunting. I'll explain it line-by-line to help you understand it better. At the top, we are creating an instance variable called **flags**. This variable holds the different render flags that we want our ground object to use when it draws the physics world. As you can see, each flag describes a different part of the physics world that we want it to draw. After creating the **flags** variable, we create two local variables called xx and yy. These variables hold the starting point for our ground generation. As we create the different ground segments, we will add and subtract from these values. We can see that the xx value is -100, which is pretty far to the left of where our room starts. This is to help make sure that we don't create the car object too close to the edge of our ground.

Now, we are ready to create our first fixture. Well, actually, you have been creating fixtures already, you just didn't do it in code. When you check the "Uses Physics" button in a new object, it tells GameMaker that you want to attach a fixture to that object. When you set the different physics properties in the object, you are actually setting the properties of the fixture that is attached to that object.

Fixtures are the physics representation of your object in the game, sort of like how sprites are the visual representation of your object in the game. The cool thing is that we can both create a fixture and set its properties using code instead of using the checkbox and filling out the physics properties fields. This gives us more control over the shape of the fixture and allows us to generate the fixture manually. In our code, you can see where we create the local variable **fix** and where we use **physics_fixture_create** and assign the id of our new fixture to the **fix** local variable. Once we have created the fixture, we can set its shape using **physics_fixture_set_chain_shape**. The chain shape allows us to add points to our fixture and it will "connect the dots", creating a chain or, in our case, the ground. There are other fixture shapes that you can use; here are their functions:

> **physics_fixture_set_polygon_shape**
> **physics_fixture_set_circle_shape**
> **physics_fixture_set_box_shape**
> **physics_fixture_set_edge_shape**
> **physics_fixture_set_chain_shape**

Our fixture shape has been set to chain. The time has come to add points to the fixture. The way we add these points will determine how rough the ground is and how good the ground looks. As you can see, I used a repeat loop statement so that we can create 100 points along our ground fixture. Inside the loop, we create the fixture point at position (xx,yy) and then we randomize the next yy point and add a slightly random value to the next xx point. We're also clamping the yy value with the median function to make sure that our points stay inside the room height.

After we create all of the points for our fixture, we set the density and restitution.

The last two things that we do are attach the fixture to our object using **physics_fixture_bind** and delete the fixture template that we created. Be aware, deleting the fixture does not delete the actual fixture that we attached to the object. It just deletes the fixture template that we have created.

Now, add a **Draw Event** and add this code to it. I talked a little bit about this function a few paragraphs back. This function should only be used as a method to debug physics, but for this example, it simplifies the concept and allows us to see the ground that we generated.

**obj_ground: Draw Event**

```
/// Draw the physics world
physics_world_draw_debug(flags);
```

You are now seconds away from having a working car physics game with randomly generated terrain. The final step is to create the room.

Create a new room and name it **rm_carworld**. Click the settings tab to set the room width to 640 and the height to 360. Click the physics tab, check "Room is Physics World", and set the "Gravity Y" vector to 30.0. Now, place the car object and the ground object in the room. Next, click on the views tab and check "Enable the use of Views" and "Visible when room starts." Set the "View In Room" w and h values to 640 and 360, respectively. Then set the "Port on Screen" w and h values to 1280 and 720, respectively.

The physics game is now ready to play! This is one of my favorite physics examples. There are a few tricky parts, but by this point in the book, you should at least have an idea of what each line of code does. Be sure to show this example off to all of your friends and family. You have worked hard and learned so much. It's time to enjoy your work a little.

# Chapter 15
# Online Multiplayer

## Foundation
There is so much to cover regarding online multiplayer. This chapter is going to be long, and even then, it will only scratch the surface of making an online game. It will, however, teach you the basics and get you started with online multiplayer. We will not be building any MMOs, but the base you receive here will help to prepare you for larger online multiplayer projects.

The first example project in this chapter only covers the absolute basics of setting up a server, a client, and the communication between them. In order to complete this first example and learn from it, you need to have a good understanding of GameMaker's data structures and their accessors (especially maps and lists) as well as the different components of an online game. I will cover the components here, but if you are struggling with the data structures, be sure to re-read Chapter 4: Arrays and Data Structures.

## Components of Online Games
There are several different ways to have online games communicate. We will be using the client-server model here. Alternatively, you can have two clients connect to each other, but I will not be covering that structure.

## Server
The *server* is generally a computer/program system that performs processing for other computers. In GameMaker, the server can be a separate program that turns your local computer into a mini server. This program will handle connections, disconnections, and data transfers to and from the different game clients. We can create a server in GameMaker Language like this.

```
var type=network_socket_tcp;
var port=8000;
max_clients=4;
server=network_create_server(type,port, max_clients);
```

The first few lines here are used to create descriptive variables that we can pass as the parameters in the `network_create_server` function. When we call the `network_create_server` function, it will return a unique id that can be used to access the created server. As you can see, we are assigning that unique id to the instance variable `server`. There are a few different options for the server type. Here they are:

```
network_socket_tcp
network_socket_udp
```

In the first edition of this book, I will only be covering `network_socket_tcp`. A UDP socket will generally be faster (it doesn't spend time error-checking the packets), but TCP is more reliable. There are many other differences, but they are beyond the scope of this chapter.

## Client

The *client* is a computer that connects to the server and (hopefully) communicates with it. Often, there will be many clients connected to one server. In GameMaker, the client is a program that connects to the server and handles messages sent from the server. It can also send messages back. This is how we can create a client in GameMaker Language and attempt to connect it to the server. Unfortunately, this won't connect yet because we haven't handled the connection on the server end. This is how we can attempt to connect from the client side.

```
var type=network_socket_tcp;
var ip="000.000.0.000";
var port=8000;
socket=network_create_socket(type);
connection=network_connect(socket,ip,port);
```

Here, we create variables for the type, IP, and port in order to make the code more readable. If you are running the server from your own computer, then you will need to get the IP address of your own computer. I will talk a little more about IP addresses, ports, and sockets in just a minute. First, look at where we call the `network_connect` function. This function will try to make a connection over a socket using a defined IP address and port. You can choose the port you would like to use, but I just use `8000`. The `network_connect` function will return a unique id that can be used to reference the connection. If the function is unable to establish a connection, it will return a number less than 0.

## Sockets
A *socket* represents a two-way connection between the client and the server. The server will actually need to keep track of multiple sockets (because it will be connected to multiple clients). You can think of the socket as the "tube" that connects the server to the client and allows data to be transferred. You have already seen how we can create the socket in the client using `network_create_socket`, but you still need to see how the server can get access to this socket as well. I'll talk more about how that is done in the actual example file.

## IPs
An *IP address* is a set of numbers that represents a unique address for a computer. The numbers are separated by periods. An IP address is similar to your physical home address, but used for computers. If you have a new friend that needs to find your home, you give your home address. If your friend's computer needs to find your computer (for example, to play a game), you give your IP address.

Of course, it is a little more complicated than that, and in this example, the connection will only work over a local network (you and your friend can play together, but you both need to be connected to the same local network). In order to get your computer's IP address, you can search "cmd" (which will run the Command Prompt) and type the command "ipconfig". This will list information about your internet configurations, including your "IPv4 Address". The IPv4 address is the one that you will want to use for this tutorial. Be aware that your router may assign you a different IP address from time to time, so you may need to update the IP address that your client uses to connect to the server.

## Ports

The *port number* is used in conjunction with your IP address. I used 8000 in this example and that should work for you. If it doesn't, you can try some different numbers. It doesn't matter too much, as long as your client and server are using the same number and there isn't any other program using your chosen port number.

## Buffers

The last term that you need to have an understanding of is *buffer*. A buffer is similar to a variable that can be sent through the socket, either from the server to the client or from the client to the server. Buffers take data in sequential order and that data is read back out of the buffer in the same order.

## Basic Example: "Create the Stars"

Now that we have gone over a few of the basic terms, you are ready for your first online game example. This is the simplest example game that I could come up with. Networking in GameMaker can be very complicated, and I want to make sure you understand the basics.

## Creating The Server

To start things off, we are going to build a basic server. In this GameMaker example, you will need to create two new project files. The first one that you create should be called **Server** and the second should be called **Client**. Once all of the code is in place, you will run the server first, and then, when you run the client, it will connect to the server.

Open up the server project once you have created it and add a new object to it. Name this object **obj_server** and add a **Create Event** to it. Drag over a **Code Action** and add this code to it:

`obj_server: Create Event`

```
/// Initialize the server object
var type=network_socket_tcp;
```

```
var port=8000;
max_clients=1;
server=network_create_server(type,port, max_clients);

socket=noone;
```

Good job! That code should look familiar to you. We are setting up the network type, the port, the maximum number of clients, and then we create the server. We are also creating an instance variable called **socket** that will store the reference to our connected client. In an example with more than one socket, you will want to create a **ds_list** to store your sockets, but for this simple example, we don't need to do that.

Now that we have created the server, we will want to make sure it is destroyed when the game ends. Add a **Game End Event** to our server object and place this code in it:

**obj_server: Game End Event**

```
/// Destroy the server
network_destroy(server);
```

Okay, up to this point, you are probably following the tutorial and thinking that it is pretty easy. Well, so far it *has been* pretty easy. Nothing too fancy and nothing you haven't seen before. Well, now things are about to get a little tricky, so pay close attention. This next bit of code will require both that you understand **ds_maps** and that you understand the terms that I went over in the start of the chapter. Don't worry though, you will get it as I step you through it.

Add an **Asynchronous Event** to the server object and select the **Networking Event** from the asynchronous submenu. This event will keep track of connections, disconnections, and data that is sent to our server. I'll show you how this works. Add this code to the event:

## obj_server: Asynchronous Networking Event

```
/// Check for the client
var type_event=async_load[? "type"];

switch(type_event){
        case network_type_connect:
                // Add the client to the socket
                if(socket==noone){
                        socket=async_load[? "socket"];
                }
                break;

        case network_type_disconnect:
                // Remove the client from the server
                socket=noone;
                break;

        case network_type_data:
                // Grab incoming data and handle it
                var buffer=async_load[? "buffer"];
                buffer_seek(buffer,buffer_seek_start,0);
                scr_received_packet(buffer);
                break;
}
```

That is a big chunk of code! Let's take it one step at a time. In the first line, we are getting a reference to the type of **Asynchronous Networking Event** that is being sent. The `async_load ds_map` is a special map created in this event only. It has all of the information that we need about the data coming in, but it cannot be accessed outside of this event. Once we get the event type, we can handle the data accordingly.

There are three types of events that could occur. The first is the **network_type_connect**. This means that a client is attempting to connect to our server. In this case, we will want to get a reference to that client; we can do that by using the `async_load ds_map` again, but instead of accessing the "type" key, we are going to access the "socket" key. This will give us a reference to the client. We just assign that information to our socket instance variable and we are done.

The second event type is the **network_type_disconnect** event. This event fires when a client disconnects from the server. This is the easiest event to handle. We are just going to set our instance variable **socket** back to **noone**.

The third, and last, event type is the **network_type_data** event. It is the most fun of the three and takes the most work, which you can see by the fact that, at the end of our case statement, we are calling a script that handles the data we get from the event. The first thing we do is create a local variable called **buffer** and assign the data from the buffer key in our **async_load ds_map** to it. Remember that buffers are like packages that contain the data that will be sent or received over the network. After getting the buffer, we want to use the **buffer_seek** function to set our read location to the start of the buffer. Data from a buffer is read in sequence. Each time you read data from the buffer, the data read is actually removed from the buffer. I'll explain this in more depth once we are ready to talk about the code contained in the script. Once we set the buffer reading location to the start, we are ready to send that information to the script. Normally, you would send the socket information as well, so that you knew which client sent the data, but because we only have one client, we don't need to worry about that in this example.

It's time to write the code in our script. Create a new script and name it **scr_received_packet**. Open up the script and type this block of code.

**scr_received_packet**

```
///scr_received_packet(buffer)
var buffer=argument[0];
// buffer is (id,x,y)

var message_id=buffer_read(buffer,buffer_u8);
// After first read buffer is now (x,y)

switch(message_id){
      case 1:
            var mx=buffer_read(buffer,buffer_u32);
            // buffer is now (y)

            var my=buffer_read(buffer,buffer_u32);
            // buffer is now empty ()
```

166

```
            //Use data from the buffer to create the click
            instance_create(mx,my,obj_mouse_click);
            break;
    }
```

I've added extra comments to help you to understand how buffer reading works. The first thing that we do is create a local variable that grabs the buffer from the argument that we passed to the script. Buffers can contain whatever we want them to. We haven't actually sent any buffers from the client yet, but I decided that our buffer will contain a message id that determines what type of message it is. Then, the x and y values are read if the message id is 1. A message id of 1, in this case, means that we want to create a mouse click object at the position of the next two pieces of data read from the buffer.

After we have read the message id from the buffer, you can see in the comment afterwards that the buffer no longer contains that information. All that is left is the x and y coordinates of the mouse click. I'm passing the id through a switch so that later, if you wanted to add other types of data that did other things, you could just pass a different id through the buffer and then add that case to the switch. Once we confirm that the message id is actually set to 1, we read both the x position and the y position from the buffer and assign those values to local variables called **mx** and **my**, respectively. You can also see by my comments that once each chunk of data is read, it is removed from the buffer (after the y value is read, there actually isn't any more information in our buffer). Once the buffer is empty, we have all of the data that we need from the client to create the mouse click object and break.

The last thing that we need to do to finish our simple server project is create the mouse click object. Add a new object and name it **obj_mouse_click**. Add a **Draw Event** to it and add these lines of code:

167

`obj_mouse_click`: Draw Event

```
/// Draw the click as a circle
draw_circle_colour(x,y,4,c_white,c_white,false);
```

This code will just draw a circle where the object is so that we can see it. Make sure to create a room and add your server object to it before you test the game.

Your first GameMaker Language server is up and ready to go! Remember that this is only the first half of the example! Even though the server is created, ready to connect to a client, and ready to receive data, we still haven't created the client that will connect to the server and then send that data when something happens.

## Creating the Client

Because this example is so basic, the client is quite a bit simpler than the server. In a more complex example, your client might be almost as complicated as the server. In a later example, I will show you how you can use one project file for both the client and the server. First, though, let's get started on our basic client.

Once you have the client project created, add a new object to it and name it **obj_client**. This client object will need a **Create Event**. Add the **Create Event**, drag over a **Code Action** and add this code block to it.

`obj_client`: Create Event

```
/// Initialize the client
var type=network_socket_tcp;
var ip="000.000.0.000";
var port=8000;
socket=network_create_socket(type);
connection=network_connect(socket,ip,port);

var size=1024;
var type=buffer_fixed;
var alignment=1;
buffer=buffer_create(size,type,alignment);
```

168

You've seen the first part of this code earlier in the chapter. We start off by defining our type, IP, and port. Once this is done, we create the socket and the connection. Once again, if you don't' know the IP address of your computer, you can use the command "ipconfig" in the command prompt and look under IPv4 to find it. After creating the socket and the connection, we create a buffer to use for sending data. We give the buffer a size of 1024 (1 kB), a type of **buffer_fixed** (this keeps the size of the buffer from changing), and an alignment of 1. The alignment refers to the byte alignment of the data. There are other buffer types, but for this example, we don't need to worry about them.

Now that our connection has been initialized and we have a buffer created and ready for communication, the time has come to actually send data. For this example, we will send data to the server when the user clicks the left mouse button somewhere in the room. Add a new **Mouse > Global > Global Left Pressed Event** to our client object and add this block of code to the event:

**obj_client: Global Left Pressed Event**

```
instance_create(mouse_x,mouse_y,obj_mouse_click);
buffer_seek(buffer,buffer_seek_start,0);

// Write the message id
buffer_write(buffer,buffer_u8,1);

// Write the mouse x position
buffer_write(buffer,buffer_u32,mouse_x);

// Write the mouse y position
buffer_write(buffer,buffer_u32,mouse_y);

network_send_packet(socket,buffer,buffer_tell(buffer));
```

The first thing that we do is create the mouse click object. We will have a mouse click object in this project that is exactly like the one in our client. This is generally not a good way to do things because you will have duplicate code, but it's okay here because this is a simple example. In the final example in this chapter, I will show you a better way to do this. Normally, you will either have one project that works as both the server

169

and the client, or you will have multiple clients connecting to the same server, which will just relay the information to and from the clients. After we create the mouse click object, we set the write position of the buffer to the very start. Then, we start writing to the buffer. The first thing that we write is the message id. Next, we write the `mouse_x` position. Finally, we write the `mouse_y` position. Like I mentioned earlier, we can send whatever data that we want and in any order in this buffer, but our server needs to know how to handle it. We already wrote the code that allows our server to handle data like this. After we have written this information to the buffer, we can use the `network_send_packet` function to send it to the server. We need to pass three arguments to this function. The first is the socket to send the data over, the next is the buffer, and the last is the size of the buffer. You can use the `buffer_tell` function to find the size of a buffer.

Our client is almost ready, but we still need to do two things. First, we need to add a **Game End Event** to the `obj_client` to make sure to destroy the dynamic data that we don't need anymore. Add the **Game End Event** and place this code in it.

**obj_client: Game End Event**

```
network_destroy(socket);
buffer_delete(buffer);
```

After that, we need to create the mouse click object in the client project as well. You can just copy the code over from the server project, but here it is again:

**obj_mouse_click: Draw Event**

```
///Draw the click as a circle
draw_circle_colour(x,y,4,c_white,c_white,false);
```

## Testing the Example

Now, we are finally ready to test this example. Make sure that there is a room in the client project and that the client object has been added to the room. Once this is done, make sure that both the server and the client projects are open. Run the server project first. We shouldn't be able to do anything in the server project, but we shouldn't get any errors. Now that the server is running, we can run the client on the same computer. Click around in the game room of the client, and make sure that the clicks are appearing in the server window as well. If everything went well, you will get one of the most exciting feelings in the world: the joy of seeing a multiplayer game that you coded running.

Getting even a basic example like this working feels great, and you should be proud of how far you have come. You will notice that if you run your client on a different computer connected to the same home network, it will still work. This example covers local area networks or LANs. If you want to use this to play a game with a friend that is connected to a different network, you can use some sort of program that allows you to set up a "fake" local area connection, or you could use your external IP address.

## Online Tic-Tac-Toe

Knowing how to send information between the server and the client is the first step, but it is important to know the limitations of this system. We want to do our best to limit the amount of information that we are sending between the client and the server. Keeping that information at a manageable size will help our game to run faster and can also help prevent "lag" in our game while the information is being sent back and forth. Have you ever been playing an online game and watched an enemy or another player object "teleport" or "jump" around on the screen because of server lag? This generally happens when the client's x and y information on that particular object fall behind the information the server has, and the server has to resynchronize the client to the server. It looks strange and is very common, even in large online titles. We want to avoid this as much as possible.

For our first online multiplayer GameMaker game, we are going to build a turn-based game. This will help us to learn how to limit the amount of data that we are sending, and we will use some other neat tricks along the way. Much of the code in this example will look familiar. This is because we are going to use a system almost exactly like the Tic-tac-toe game in the Data Structures chapter. This should make it easier for you to separate the actual game code from the online code (which we will add on top of it).

Let's start! First off, add a sprite called **spr_mark**. Give the sprite a size of 64 × 64. Add two subimages to the sprite. The first subimage will be our "O", and the second subimage will be our "X". Once we have the sprite, add a new background as well. Name the background **bg_space**, give it a size of 64 × 64, and draw a box outline that fills up the entire background. We will use nine of these backgrounds in our room to create the Tic-tac-toe board. Make sure you check "use as tileset" and set both the "Tile Width" and "Tile Height" to 64. Here is a screenshot of both the sprite and the background:

**Sprite: spr_mark**

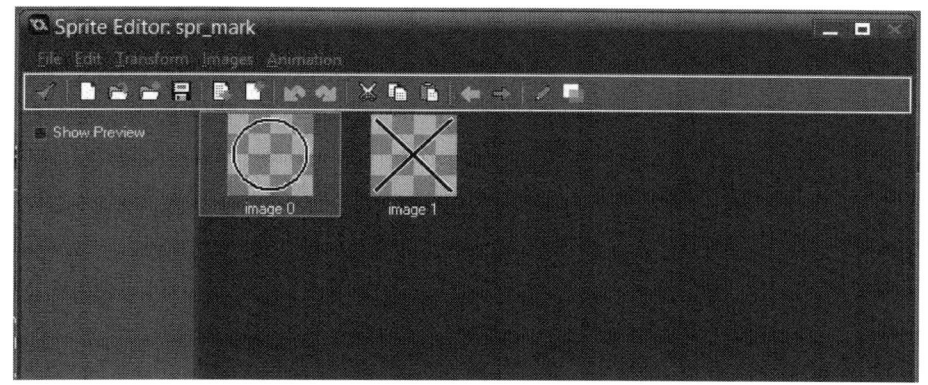

**Background: bg_space**

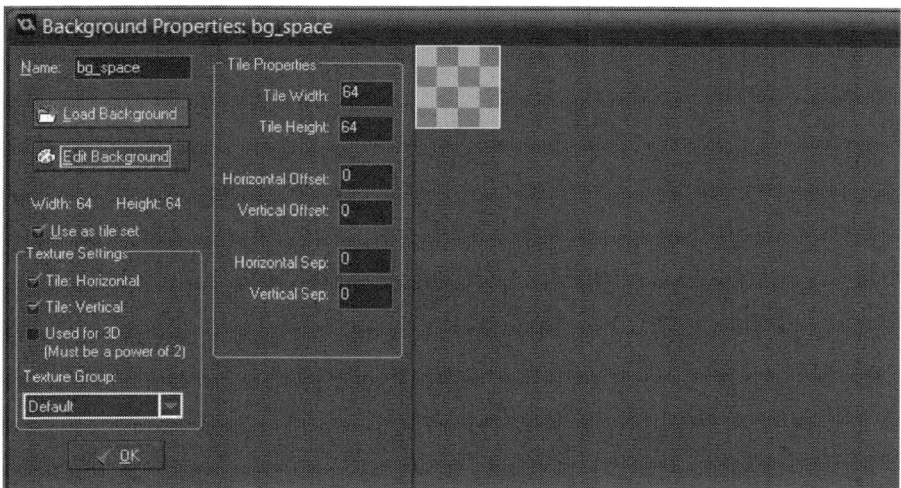

Now that we have the background and sprite ready, create a new room. Name the room **rm_board**. Set its width to 192 and its height to 224. Now,

172

go to the tiles tab and use the background we created to make your Tic-Tac-Toe board. When you are finished, your room should look something like this. I placed the tiles lower in the room to leave some room for information at the top of the game window.

**Room: rm_board**

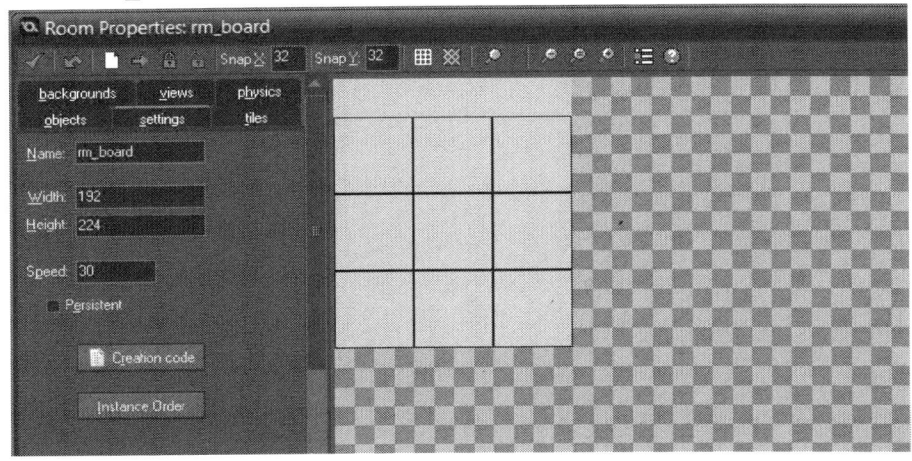

The next step, before adding our objects, is to set up some macros. Open up the "All configurations" macro list and add these macros and corresponding values.

**PLACE_MARK: 0**
**BLANK_MARK: -1**
**O_MARK: 0**
**X_MARK: 1**
**CELL_SIZE: 64**

When we are done, the macro list should look like this:

173

## All Configurations Macro List

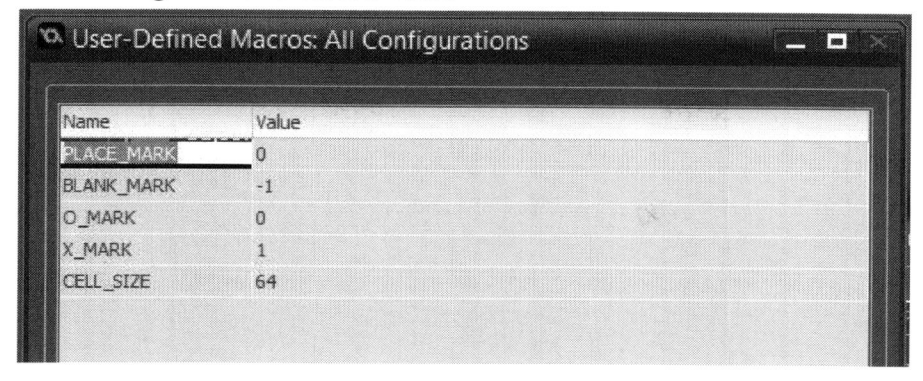

| Name | Value |
|---|---|
| PLACE_MARK | 0 |
| BLANK_MARK | -1 |
| O_MARK | 0 |
| X_MARK | 1 |
| CELL_SIZE | 64 |

The time has come to start adding objects and their events/actions. Create two new objects. Name the first one **obj_network** and the second one **obj_game**. These two objects are all that we need to control the entire game.

- obj_network
- obj_game

Start by opening up the network object, adding a **Create Event** to it, and dragging a **Code Action** into the event. The **Code Action** will contain this code:

### obj_network: Create Event

```
/// Initialize the network
var type=network_socket_tcp;
var ip="000.000.0.000";
var port=8000;
socket=network_create_socket(type);
connection=network_connect(socket,ip,port);
is_server=false;
global.turn='other';

if (connection<0) {
        global.turn='mine';
        max_clients=1;
        server=network_create_server(type,port, max_clients);
        network_destroy(socket);
        is_server=true;
```

174

```
        client=noone;
}
```

This bit of code is clever because it allows us to use the same game project for both the server and the client. We start by creating a socket and a connection. Then, we set two variables. The first variable is an instance variable called `is_server`. At first, we assume that this game is the client. Because we are the client, we set `global.turn` to true.

If `network_connect` is unable to establish a connection (for example, if a server doesn't exist), then the function returns a number less than 0. We can use this to test if there is already a server. If there isn't already a server (`if (connection<0)`), then we need to create one.

Creating the server is easy. We set the `global.turn` to "mine", set the `max_clients` to 1, and call `network_create_server` to create our server with the information that we have already established. Because we aren't a client, we don't need the socket we created anymore, so we destroy it. Then, we set `is_server` to true and `client` to noone.

We need to add a **Game End Event** to make sure that we destroy our socket or server. The one we destroy will depend on whether or not we are a server. Add a **Game End Event** and put this code in it:

`obj_network`: Game End Event

```
/// Clean up dynamic data
if (is_server) {
        network_destroy(server);
} else {
        network_destroy(socket);
}
```

This is a small code block. We check to see if we are a server. If we are, we destroy the server; if not, we destroy the (client) socket.

Add an **Asynchronous > Networking Event**. This event will fire anytime the server picks up a message from the client. There are three types of messages that will be sent: an attempt to connect, an attempt to disconnect, and actual data. We will check for each of these types and handle them accordingly. Drag over a **Code Action** and add this code block to it:

**obj_network: Networking Event**

```
var type_event=async_load[? "type"];
switch(type_event) {
        case network_type_connect:
                if (!is_server) break;

                // Get a reference to the client's socket
                if (client==noone) {
                        client=async_load[? "socket"];
                }
                break;

        case network_type_disconnect:
                if (!is_server) break;

                // Remove the reference to the client's socket
                client=noone;
                break;

        case network_type_data:
                // Handle the data received
                var buffer=async_load[? "buffer"];
                buffer_seek(buffer, buffer_seek_start,0);
                scr_handle_packet(buffer);
                break;
}
```

The first thing that we do is grab a reference to the type of event that is being sent. If it is a connect event or a disconnect event and we are not the server, we just break out and ignore them. If we *are* the server, we make sure to add the new client when they are connecting and remove them when they are disconnecting. For the data event, it doesn't matter if we are the server or the client, both can send and receive data. When we know that we are receiving data, we create a local variable to store the buffer.

176

The buffer is the data structure that the data is contained in. We call **buffer_seek** to make sure that the buffer starts reading from the start. Then, we pass the buffer into a script that will handle the data.

Before we create that script, we are going to finish up the network object by adding a **Draw Event** to it. This **Draw Event** will draw some information about the game on the screen. We are going to draw the turn and some text telling the player that they are the client or the server. Drag over a **Code Action**. This is the code we will add to it:

**obj_network: Draw Event**

```
/// Draw the game information
draw_text(2,0,"Turn: "+global.turn);
var player_text='';
if (is_server) {
        player_text='Player X Mark';
} else {
        player_text='Player O Mark';
}
draw_text(2,16,player_text);
```

This code draws the turn to the screen and then checks to see if the player is a server. If so, it sets the player text to tell the player that they are the X mark. If they aren't the server, it sets the player text to tell the player that they are the O mark.

Now that we have finished up with the network object, let's write the script it uses. Add a new script and name it **scr_handle_packet**.

- **scr_handle_packet**

This is the block of code we will write in the script:

**scr_handle_packet**

```
///scr_handle_packet(buffer)
var buffer=argument[0];
var message_id=buffer_read(buffer,buffer_u8);
```

```
switch(message_id) {
    case PLACE_MARK:
        // Read from the buffer
        var gridx=buffer_read(buffer, buffer_u8);
        var gridy=buffer_read(buffer, buffer_u8);

        // Set the mark
        obj_game.grid[# gridx, gridy]=!is_server;

        // Start my turn
        global.turn='mine';
        break;
}
```

It is important to know how the buffer is organized. For this game, I decided to organize the buffer like this: (message id, x position, y position). You can choose to organize the buffer in any way you wish. You organize the buffer when you actually send it, and you will see that part here soon. We start by getting a local reference to the buffer. Then, we read from the buffer to get the message id. We actually don't need a message id (the *message id* is used to indicate what kind of information the buffer contains) for this game because we are only sending one type of data, but I designed it this way so that if you wanted to add other systems to the game (e.g., chat functionality), it would be easy to create new message ids and handle those message types accordingly.

Now that we have the message id, we can switch through the different message id possibilities. I've stored the only message id that is possible in this game in a macro. This makes the code more readable. If the message id from the buffer matches the message id in that macro, we will step into the code after that case. Once we are in that section of code, we read the x position and the y position from the buffer and store those in local variables.

At this point, we have all the information that we need from the other player to update our game board. We can use a shortcut here because of the way the grid is set up. In our grid (you may remember from the first time we made a Tic-tac-toe game), X marks are represented by a 1 and O marks are represented by a 0. The server always uses X marks. If we are the

178

server and we receive a mark from the client, we know that the mark should be a 0. The `is_server` will return a 1 (true) if we are the server, so if we use the not operator on it (`!is_server`), it will return a 0. If we are *not* the server, then `is_server` will return a 0. If we use the not operator on it (`!is_server`), then it will return a 1. This is a sneaky trick that allows us to place the correct mark regardless of whether we are the server or the client.

The final step of this code changes the turn back to the current player's turn. If we are receiving a "mark this spot" message from the other player, it is currently the other player's turn. Once we mark their spot, we can switch the turn back to us.

It is finally time to write the game object's code. Open up **obj_game** and add a new **Create Event** to it. Like I said before, much of this code will look familiar, but we are going to change a few things, so pay close attention. Drag over a **Code Action** and add this code to it:

**obj_game: Create Event**

```
/// Create the ds grid and initialize the game object
grid=ds_grid_create(3,3);
ds_grid_set_region(grid,0,0,2,2,BLANK_MARK);
```

This block of code is simple enough. All we do is create the grid and set all of the cells in the grid to the **BLANK_MARK** value. **BLANK_MARK** is a macro that we created earlier; it contains the value of -1.

Before we do the mouse click event and its message-sending magic, let's add a **Draw Event** to the object and put this code in it:

**obj_game: Draw Event**

```
/// Draw the game board
for (var i=0; i<ds_grid_width(grid); i++) {
        for (var j=0; j<ds_grid_height(grid); j++) {
                if (grid[# i, j]==BLANK_MARK) continue;
                var subimage=grid[# i, j];
```

```
                    var mx=i*CELL_SIZE;
                    var my=(i*CELL_SIZE)+32;
                    draw_sprite(spr_mark,subimage,mx,my);
        }
}
```

This **Draw Event** is almost identical to the one that we used in the previous Tic-tac-toe example game. We loop through the different cells in the grid. If the cell is empty, we use the continue statement to skip it, because we only need to draw cells that contain marks. For all of the other cells, we create three local variables, one for the subimage (which conveniently correlates to the value that we stored in the grid), one for the mark's x position, and one for the mark's y position. Then, we draw the sprite `spr_mark` using the subimage and position data that we gathered.

Add a new **Mouse > Global > Global Left Pressed Event**. This event will hold the code that handles the logic for setting a mark and sending that new mark information to the other player. Drag over a **Code Action** block and add this code:

**obj_game: Global Left Pressed Event**

```
/// Mark the board
if (global.turn=='mine') {
        // Grab the mouse position and convert it to the grid
        var gridx=mouse_x div CELL_SIZE;
        var gridy=(mouse_y-32) div CELL_SIZE;

        // Make sure the square isn't already taken
        if (grid[# gridx, gridy]!=BLANK_MARK) exit;

        // Set the mark
        grid[# gridx, gridy] obj_network.is_server;

        // Send the action over the network
        var buffer=buffer_create(1024,buffer_fixed,1);
        buffer_seek(buffer,buffer_seek_start,0);
        buffer_write(buffer,buffer_u8,PLACE_MARK);
        buffer_write(buffer,buffer_u8,gridx);
        buffer_write(buffer,buffer_u8,gridy);
```

180

```
            var receiver=noone;
            if (obj_network.is_server) {
                    receiver=obj_network.client;
            } else {
                    receiver=obj_network.socket;
            }
            network_send_packet(receiver,buffer,buffer_tell(buffer));
            buffer_delete(buffer);
            global.turn='other';
    }
```

The first thing we do is make sure it is our turn. If it isn't our turn, then we shouldn't be able to place a mark. After making sure it is our turn, we grab the mouse's position and convert it into cell coordinates on our grid using the division operator.

After getting that information, we check to make sure that there isn't already a mark in that spot and mark the board on our side of the connection.

Now, we need to send this new information to the other player across the network connection. We start by creating a buffer and adding the message id, the mark's x position, and the mark's y position. Then, we use the **is_server** property of the network object to determine who the receiver will be. After getting all that ready, we send the buffer using **network_send_packet**, delete the buffer using **buffer_delete**, and change the turn so that it is the other player's turn.

The final step is to add both your network object and your game object to the room.

## Testing your Multiplayer Tic-Tac-Toe Game

Congratulations! You finished your very first online multiplayer game. The easiest way to test your game is to create an executable of your project by going to File > Create Application, then change the file type to "Single runtime executable" and press Save. After your project builds, you can run the game twice and two game windows will pop up. You should be able to play Tic-tac-toe against yourself.

If you want to test it further, you can copy the executable file onto another computer and make sure that the connection still works.

# Chapter 16
# Artificial Intelligence

## Enemies
The main difference between artificial intelligence (AI) objects and player objects is their inputs. The player object is controlled by the mouse, keyboard, or gamepad. The AI objects are often controlled based on distance, collision, and visibility checks.

## Top-Down Game Example
Let's look at a simple method for programming artificial intelligence in a top-down game. We will use a simple state system with some distance checks to accomplish this task. First, let's start by creating some filler sprites. Create two new sprites and name them **spr_enemy** and **spr_player**.

- `spr_enemy`
- `spr_player`

I just made them both 32 x 32 circles. My player is blue and my enemy is red. After creating these two sprites, we need to create two new objects. Name them **obj_enemy** and **obj_player**.

- `obj_enemy`
- `obj_player`

Open up the player object and add a **Create Event** to the object. Inside this **Create Event**, add a **Code Action** and place this simple code inside.

`obj_player: Create Event`

```
/// Initialize the player
hp=1;
```

We are setting the **hp** variable to 1 for the sake of simplicity. We will use the **image_alpha** property of the player object to show how much health the player has left. Because this property only goes from 0 to 1, it suits our purposes to set the health to 1 as well. After finishing up the code in the **Create Event**, add a **Step Event** to our **obj_player**. Drag a **Code Action** into the **Step Event** and type this code in the action.

`obj_player: Step Event`

```
/// Control the player's movement
var right=keyboard_check(vk_right);
var left=keyboard_check(vk_left);
var up=keyboard_check(vk_up);
var down=keyboard_check(vk_down);

if (right) {
        x+=4;
}

if (left) {
        x-=4;
}

if (up) {
        y-=4;
}

if (down) {
        y+=4;
}

image_alpha=hp;
if (hp<=0) {
        game_end();
}
```

This block of code allows the player to move and causes the game to end when the player's hp variable is less than or equal to 0. It also sets the `image_alpha` property equal to the value of the player's hp. As the hp value decreases, so will the `image_alpha` property. This will cause the player to become more transparent as he/she loses health.

Now, the player object is done. There really wasn't anything too tricky there, and most of that code should look very familiar to you by now. Let's move on the the fun part of this example, creating the artificial intelligence for the enemy.

Open up the enemy object and add a new **Create Event** to it. Inside this **Create Event**, we are going to add a **Code Action** and create some variables inside that action. Here is the code we will add:

**obj_enemy: Create Event**

```
/// Initialize the enemy
state_text='idle';
state=scr_enemy_idle;
sight_range=choose(96,128,180);
attack_range=24;
spd=3;
```

These variables will be used to control our artificial intelligence. The first variable, `state_text`, is only used for debugging purposes. This will allow us to draw the current state of the enemy. The next variable, `state`, will store a script that controls the behavior of each state. As you can see, we are setting this variable equal to `scr_enemy_idle`. We do this because we want all of our enemies to start out in the idle state. The third variable, `sight_range`, will hold either 96, 128, or 180. These numbers represent the distance our enemy will be able to see the player from. The **choose** function will select a random number from the three values passed to it, causing each enemy to have a slightly different sight range. The fourth variable, `attack_range`, is the distance that our enemies will be able to attack from. The last variable, **spd**, will contain the value of the movement speed for each enemy. We are making the value 3, which is slower than our player. This allows our player to escape from the enemies.

185

Now that the **Create Event** is finished, it is time to add a **Step Event** to our enemy. This **Step Event** will contain a **Code Action** with this bit of code.

**obj_enemy: Step Event**

```
/// Control the states
script_execute(state);
```

This line is simple enough. We use the **script_execute** function to run whatever script is assigned to our state variable. This is a clean and easy way to manage the states of our enemy object.

In order to make the game feel a bit cooler, and for you to be able to visualize how this artificial intelligence works, we are going to add some neat code into the enemy object's **Draw Event**. Add a new **Draw Event** to the enemy object and drag over a **Code Action**. Here is the code you will place in that action:

**obj_enemy: Draw Event**

```
/// Draw self and state
draw_set_halign(fa_center);
draw_set_valign(fa_middle);
draw_self();
draw_set_alpha(.1);
draw_circle_colour(x,y,sight_range,c_red,c_red,false);
draw_set_alpha(1);
draw_text(x,y,state_text);
```

Now that we are drawing the enemy and its sight range, we are ready to write the scripts controlling its different states. The first script that we write will control the idle state. Add a new script and name it **scr_enemy_idle**.

**scr_enemy_idle**

```
///scr_enemy_idle()
state_text='idle';
```

```
var dis=point_distance(x,y,obj_player.x,obj_player.y);
if (dis<=sight_range) {
        state=scr_enemy_chase;
}
```

The script for the idle state isn't too complicated. We make sure to change the state text variable (for debugging). Then, we get the distance to the player. If that distance to the player is less than or equal to our sight range, then we can change to the chase state.

We are using the chase state, but we actually haven't created the script for that state yet. Let's do that now. Add a new script and name it **scr_enemy_chase**.

### scr_enemy_chase

```
///scr_enemy_chase()
state_text='chase';
var dis=point_distance(x,y,obj_player.x,obj_player.y);
var dir=point_direction(x,y,obj_player.x,obj_player.y);

if (dis<=sight_range && dis>attack_range) {
        motion_set(dir,spd);
} else if (dis<=attack_range) {
        speed=0;
        direction=0;
        state=scr_enemy_attack;
} else {
        speed=0;
        direction=0;
        state=scr_enemy_idle;
}
```

The chase state script starts like the idle script, by setting the **state_text** variable. After that, we get temporary references to the distance from (and the direction to) the player. Next, we add some if statements to check to see whether we are within the sight range, within the attack range, or outside both ranges for our enemy. If we are within the sight range, we continue moving towards the player. If we are within the attack range, we stop moving and switch to the attack state. If we are outside both ranges, then we stop moving and switch back to the idle state.

Lastly, we need to write the code that will be in the attack script. Add a new script and name it `scr_enemy_attack`.

**scr_enemy_attack**

```
///scr_enemy_attack()
state_text='attack';
var dis=point_distance(x,y,obj_player.x,obj_player.y);

if (dis>attack_range) {
        state=scr_enemy_chase;
} else {
        // Attack
        if (alarm[0]==-1) {
                obj_player.hp-=0.1;
                alarm[0]=30;
        }
}
```

With the attack script, we set the `state_text` variable and get a temporary distance reference from the player. After that, we check the distance. If we are outside the attack range, we swap back to the chase state. If the player is within the attack range, we can subtract from the player's hp by 0.1; we are also using an alarm to make sure that the attack doesn't happen every step. If it did, our player would die in less than a second. Using this alarm forces the enemy to only attack once every second.

In order to use the alarm, we have to add the **Alarm Event** to the enemy object. It doesn't actually need to have any code in the event because we are controlling the alarm inside of our attack script. We do still need to add the event and add a **Code Action** or comment because GameMaker automatically removes events that don't have any actions in them. Let's add a new **Alarm 0 Event** to the object enemy and drag over a **Code Action**. In the action, type this:

`obj_enemy: Alarm 0 Event`

```
/// This is just a comment in a code action to prevent
// GameMaker from removing the event.
```

Now, both our player and our enemy objects are ready. Create a new room, add a few enemies to it, and add a player. Make sure that you have assigned the `spr_enemy` sprite to the enemy object and the `spr_player` spite to the player object. Once the objects have been added to the new room, run the game and test it. Watch the behavior of the enemies.

This simple artificial intelligence example teaches the basics of using a state system for enemy AI. This is a great place to start, and we have already come so far. Great work! Try to think of one more state that we could add to these enemies that would make them more interesting. It might be fun to try adding a wandering state that makes the enemies wander around between periods in the idle state. Play around with it and have fun!

## Platform Artificial Intelligence

Platform games can be tricky for beginners, especially when it comes to the enemies and their artificial intelligence. I will describe two common forms of platform artificial intelligence in the next section, and I'm going to teach you how both of them work.

## Back and Forth Enemies

Many platform games have a basic enemy that simply moves back and forth in some area of space. These enemies don't aggressively seek out the player but act as a moving hazard that the player must avoid or deal with. Most of the time, these enemies only turn around when they encounter a ledge or a wall. There are many ways to program enemies like this. One method uses invisible objects placed in the room that, when collided with, cause the enemy to turn around. This method is straightforward and easy to program. It does make it harder to build each level, though, because the designer has to worry about placing two of these objects for every single enemy that they want to add to the room. We are going to look at a different way that allows the enemies to be slightly smarter and detect (by themselves) when they should turn around.

Before we start programming, we need to create two sprites and two corresponding objects. Create two new sprites and name them `spr_enemy` and `spr_solid`.

- `spr_enemy`
- `spr_solid`

For this example, I made my enemy sprite a red box with a size of 32 x 32 and my solid sprite a 32 x 32 gray box. Center the origin for the enemy sprite, but not for the solid sprite. Here is an image of both of my sprites and their properties:

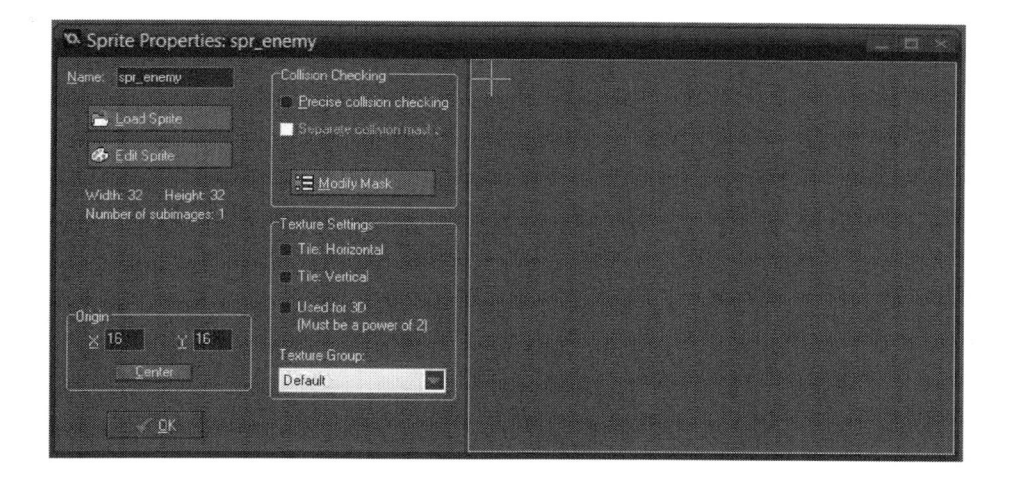

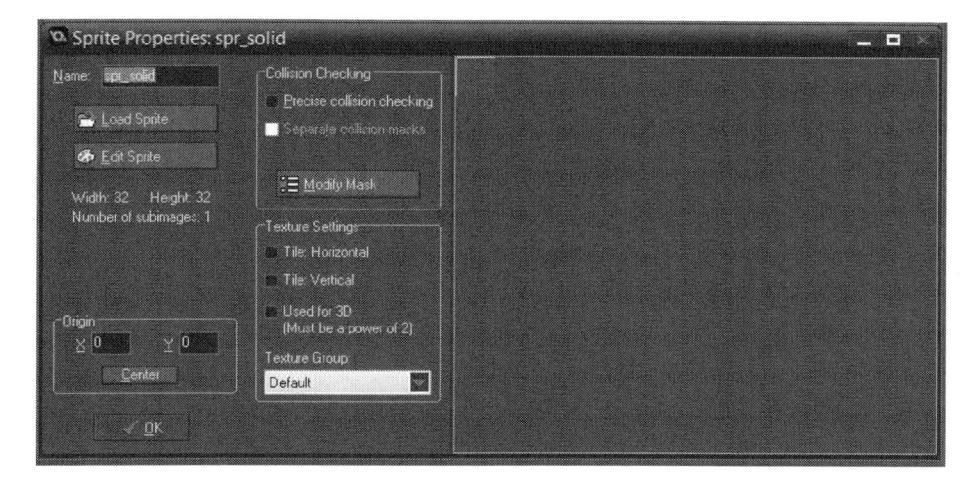

Now create two objects and name them **obj_enemy** and **obj_solid**.

- **obj_enemy**
- **obj_solid**

These will be the only two objects that we need for now. We don't need to add any events or code actions to the solid object, but you should create a room and build a simple platformer level. Once you have built a basic level, you can add a few enemy objects to it. Here is a screenshot of the level that I built.

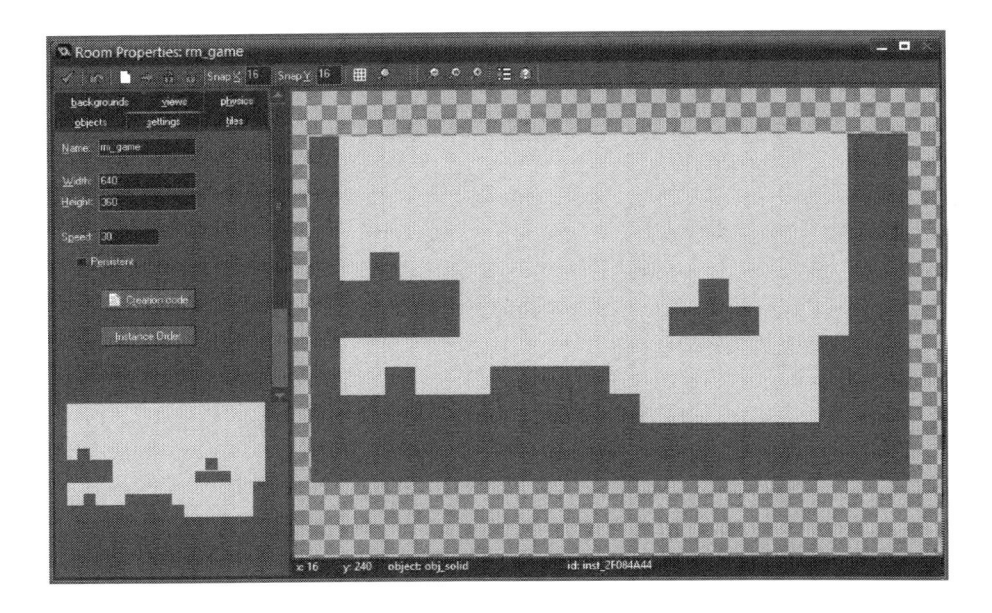

Now that the room, objects, and sprites are ready, we can start adding the events and code actions needed for our basic back-and-forth platform enemies.

Open up the enemy object and add a **Create Event** to it. Now drag over a **Code Action** and add this small block of code in it:

**obj_enemy: Create Event**

```
/// Set the initial state of the object
state=choose(scr_enemy_move_right,scr_enemy_move_left);
```

191

In this line of code, we are using the **choose** function to pick one of the two scripts and assign it to our enemy object's state variable. We haven't created these scripts yet, but we will shortly.

Now we need to add a **Step Event** to the enemy that executes our current state. Here is the code that we will use:

**obj_enemy: Step Event**

```
/// Execute the state
script_execute(state);
```

The two easy parts are done now. It's time to create the two scripts that we will be using to control the enemy's movements. Create two new scripts. Name them **scr_enemy_move_right** and **scr_enemy_move_left**.

- scr_enemy_move_right
- scr_enemy_move_left

For this code, we need to check two things. We need to find out whether the space to the right is free of any solid objects. The other thing that we need to check is whether the section *under* the space to the right of us is a ledge or not. Open up **scr_enemy_move_right** and add this code to it.

**scr_enemy_move_right**

```
///scr_enemy_move_right
var right_free=!place_meeting(x+2,y,obj_solid);
var xpos=x+(sprite_width/2)+1;
var ypos=y+(sprite_height/2)+1;
var no_ledge=instance_position(xpos,ypos,obj_solid);

if (right_free && no_ledge) {
        x+=2;
} else {
        state=scr_enemy_move_left;
}
```

192

We use the `place_meeting` function to check for any objects to the right of us. If there aren't any, then `right_free` will be set to true. We use `instance_position` to check whether there is a ledge to the right of us. If there isn't a ledge, `no_ledge` will be set to true. We use an if statement to check both of our temporary variables. If `right_free` is true and `no_ledge` is true, we can move the the right. If not, we change the state to start moving to the left.

Open `scr_enemy_move_left` and add this code to it. The codes are very similar, the only difference being the direction for the checks and movement.

### scr_enemy_move_left

```
///scr_enemy_move_left
var right_free=!place_meeting(x-2,y,obj_solid);
var xpos=x-sprite_width/2)-1;
var ypos=y+(sprite_height/2)+1;
var no_ledge=instance_position(xpos,ypos,obj_solid);

if (right_free && no_ledge) {
        x-=2;
} else {
        state=scr_enemy_move_left;
}
```

I'm not going to explain the code in this script because it works almost exactly like the other script.

## Test Your Artificial Intelligence

After creating both of these scripts, we should be able to run our game and watch the enemies move back and forth.

## Smarter Enemies

Congratulations! You have created your very first platform artificial intelligence. The enemies you created are common in many platform games, but once the player has figured out their timing, they are easy to avoid. For one more example, we are going to add to the previous example and create a platform enemy that attempts to chase the cursor around the level.

For this smarter enemy, we will need to add better collision checking and gravity. The enemy will only have one state but that state will be more complicated than the states of the simple enemy. Add a new object to the game and name it **obj_smarter_enemy**.

- **obj_smarter_enemy**

We can use the same sprite used for the first enemy, or we might use a sprite of a slightly different color. Add a **Create Event** to the new object and place this code inside the event.

**obj_smarter_enemy: Create Event**

```
/// Initialize the smarter enemy
hspd=0;
vspd=0;
grav=1;
jspd=14;
state=scr_chase_mouse;
```

We create quite a few instance variables here, and we will be using these different variables to control our object. We have a horizontal speed, a vertical speed, a gravity amount, a jump amount, and our state.

Add a new **Step Event**. This event will control the state, the collisions, and the gravity.

**obj_smarter_enemy: Step Event**

```
/// Control the state and collisions
script_execute(state);

// Gravity
if (!place_meeting(x,y+1,obj_solid)) {
       vspd+=grav;
}

// Horizontal collisions
if (place_meeting(x+hspd,y,obj_solid)) {
```

194

```
            hspd=0;
    }

    // Move horizontally
    x+=hspd;

    // Vertical collisions
    if (place_meeting(x,y+vspd,obj_solid)) {
            while (!place_meeting(x,y+sign(vspd),obj_solid)) {
                    y+=sign(vspd);
            }
            vspd=0;
    }

    // Move vertically
    y+=vspd;
```

The first part of this code runs our current state. After that, we check for a solid under the enemy and apply gravity if there isn't something solid there. In the middle section, we set our horizontal speed to 0 if there is a collision horizontally. After the collision check, we apply the horizontal movement speed to the enemy's x position. Lastly, we check for vertical collisions. Because the vertical movement has a speed that could change (due to gravity), we need to make this collision check smarter. We use a while statement to move the enemy object up against solid objects in the vertical axis. Then we apply the vertical speed to the y position.

The last thing that we need to do in order to get our smarter artificial intelligence moving is write the **scr_enemy_chase** script. Add a new script and add this code to it.

**scr_enemy_chase**

```
    ///scr_chase_mouse()
    if (point_distance(x,y,mouse_x,y)>16) {
            if (x<mouse_x) {
                    hspd=4;
            } else {
                    hspd=-4;
            }
```

195

```
    } else {
            hspd=0;
    }

    // Set up check variables
    var on_ground=place_meeting(x,y+1,obj_solid);
    var mouse_above=(mouse_y<y);
    var wall=place_meeting(x+hspd,y,obj_solid);
    var xpos=x+sign(hspd);
    var ypos=y+(sprite_height/2)+1;
    var ledge=!instance_position(xpos,ypos,obj_solid);

    // Check for jump
    if (on_ground && mouse_above && (wall || ledge)) {
            vspd=-jspd;
    }
```

The first check in our chase script is our distance from the mouse position. After that, we see if we are to the left or the right of the mouse. If we are to the left, we move right, and if we are to the right, we move left. That part is rather simple.

Deciding when the enemy object needs to jump is a slightly more complicated segment. We start by setting up our different checks. We use **place_meeting** to see whether we are on the ground. We use the mouse's y position to see if we are above or below it. We use **place_meeting** to check our movement direction to see if there is a wall.

Finally, we use some position checks and **instance_position** to see if there is an edge. Once all of our check variables are set up, we can write the if statement that checks our different conditions. We use the **and** operator to make sure that we are on the ground and that the mouse is actually above us. If those two cases are true, we use the **or** operator to check if there is a wall or an edge. In both of these cases, our enemy will jump.

## Testing Your Smarter Enemy

Make sure you have added the new enemy to the room, then run the game. The enemy should make an attempt to chase the cursor around the room. The artificial intelligence isn't perfect, but it works quite well for most situations.

## Pathfinding in a Maze

One of the other topics that I will teach you is how to make an enemy that is smart enough to navigate a maze. GameMaker does a good job of simplifying this process for you, but there are still a few things that can be confusing for people who have never done it before. I'm going to show you how to harness this amazing feature of GameMaker Studio and teach you some tips that will help you to avoid pitfalls that you might encounter.

## The Enemy in a Maze Example

Let's start to set up our pathfinding. Open up a new GameMaker project and add two new sprites to it. These two sprites will be named **spr_enemy** and **spr_solid**. Center the enemy sprite, but leave the origin of the solid sprite at 0,0.

- spr_enemy
- spr_solid

I made both of my sprites simple boxes with dimensions of 32 x 32. After creating these sprites, add 3 new objects to the game. Name them **obj_enemy**, **obj_solid**, and **obj_grid**.

- obj_enemy
- obj_solid
- obj_grid

Assign the enemy sprite to the enemy object and the solid sprite to the solid object; leave the grid object without any assigned sprite. Create a basic room and give it a height of 640 and a width of 360. We can name the room whatever we like, but I named mine **rm_maze**. Add in the grid object, the enemy object, and create a maze in the room using the solid object to form the walls. Be sure to keep the wall-section objects (**obj_solid**) snapped to a 32 x 32 grid. Here is a screenshot of my room:

197

My solid objects are the dark gray ones and my enemy object is the red one. Once the room is complete, we are ready to start programming. Open up the grid object and add a new **Create Event** to it. Place this code in the **Create Event**:

**obj_grid: Create Event**

```
/// Using an alarm, wait one step, then create the grid
alarm[0]=1;
```

The reason we are using an alarm here before creating the grid is to make sure that all of the solid instances have been created. We need them to be in the room before creating the grid and then adding the solid objects to the grid. There are other ways to do this (changing the creation order of your instances in the room), but this method will work for this example.

Now, add the **Alarm 0 Event**. In this event, we will be creating the grid that GameMaker will use for the pathfinding. Once we have created the grid and added the solid objects to the grid, GameMaker can use that information to create a path between two defined points in the grid.

### obj_grid: Alarm 0 Event

```
/// Create the grid
// Create some temporary variables
var cw=32;
var ch=32;
var hc=room_width/cw;
var vc=room_height/ch;

// Create the grid
global.grid=mp_grid_create(0,0,hc,vc,cw,ch);

// Add the walls to the grid
mp_grid_add_instances(global.grid,obj_solid,0);
```

First, we set up some temporary variables that we will use to pass to the **mp_grid_create** function. The **cw** and **ch** variables stand for the cell width and the cell height, respectively. Keeping these numbers as large as possible (while still ensuring that the enemy movement looks good) will reduce the likelihood of performance issues in your game. The **hc** and **vc** variables stand for the horizontal cell count and the vertical cell count, respectively. We calculate these numbers based on the room dimensions and the cell dimensions we are using. Now, we are read to create the grid. The first two arguments in our **mp_grid_create** function are the starting **x** and starting **y** position for the grid. The next two are the horizontal cell count and the vertical cell count. Lastly, we have the cell width and the cell height. Once we have created the grid, we need to add the solid objects to the grid to make sure that GameMaker knows that those objects should be counted as walls (which the enemy cannot walk through). We use the **mp_gird_add_instances** to accomplish this task. It takes three arguments: the grid we created, the instance to add, and whether or not to check precisely for that instance. A precise check will use precise collision checking on the sprite of the object passed in. Our solid object is just a box, so we don't need to worry about precise collision checking.

Now that the grid has been created, we need to make sure that we don't end up with any memory leaks: we need to add a **Game End Event**, which will destroy the grid when the game is closed.

## obj_grid: Game End Event

```
/// Destroy the grid
mp_grid_destroy(global.grid);
```

We use the **mp_grid_destroy** function and pass the grid as an argument in order to destroy it.

Good news! Your grid object is finished and the **global.grid** variable is ready to be used in our enemy's smart pathfinding. Now, we just need to program the enemy. Surprisingly, because of the way GameMaker handles AI pathfinding, it is actually even easier than setting up the grid. We will program our enemy to move to a location in the maze that the user clicks on. Open up the enemy object and add a new **Create Event** to it.

## obj_enemy: Create Event

```
/// Create the path
path=path_add();
```

Here, we are using the **path_add** function to create a new path and assign it to the **path** instance variable. We will use this later when the user clicks a location in the maze.

Now add a new **Mouse > Global Mouse > Left Pressed Event** to our enemy object and place this segment of code in it:

## obj_enemy: Global Left Pressed Event

```
/// Find the mouse click and move towards it along a path
var mx=(mouse_x div 32)*32+16;
var my=(mouse_y div 32)*32+16;

if (mp_grid_path(global.grid,path,x,y,mx,my,1)) {
        path_start(path,4,path_action_stop,false);
}
```

First, we get a grid-snapped version of the mouse's **x** and **y** position. Once we have that, we use the `mp_grid_path` function inside of an if condition to determine if a suitable path was found. The `mp_grid_path` function takes seven arguments. The first argument is the grid to use to check for a suitable path, the second is the path that the function will use to create a movement solution, the third and fourth are the starting position of the path (we use the enemy object's **x** and **y** position), the fifth and sixth are the end position of the path (we use the mouse's **x** and **y** position), and the final argument is a boolean value that determines if the object can move at 45° angles in the path. We set this to true. If the `mp_grid_path` function is able to find a solution, we will enter into the block of our if statement and start moving along the path that we have created. To move on this path and determine what action occurs when the object reaches its destination, we use the `path_start` function. For the first argument of this function, we pass the id of the path to use. Next, we pass the speed at which the enemy object should move along the path. After that, we pass the action that should be performed at the end of the path; `path_action_stop` will stop the enemy when it reaches the end. Finally, we pass a boolean that tells the function whether or not the path is relative to the object or to the room. A value of `false` indicates that the path will be relative to the room and that works just great for our example.

Once again, congratulations! Run the game and test your enemy. If you click on an area of the room that is possible for the enemy to reach, it should, very cleverly, move along the shortest path until it reaches that point. If you want to learn more about how GameMaker accomplishes this task, you can research the A* algorithm.

Now, you have one more weapon in your arsenal of artificial intelligence tactics, and you can make your enemies even smarter!

# Experiment with Artificial Intelligence

Hopefully this chapter has taught you a few different tricks for artificial intelligence and you now have some ideas of your own or even ideas on how to improve the examples in this chapter. Keep in mind, smart artificial intelligence doesn't always make your game fun; sometimes, if the artificial intelligence is too good, then the game isn't enjoyable. Have fun with your enemies, but remember that your game is the most fun when the artificial intelligence is challenging, not punishing. And often, you can have them be challenging with very simple artificial intelligence.

# Final Info
# Contact and Kickstarter

## My Contact Information
If you have any questions or concerns, don't hesitate to contact me! The best way to contact me is by email, but I will list my other profiles as well. Be sure to check out my YouTube Channel for free tutorial videos on GameMaker Studio.

**Email:** heartbeast.studios@gmail.com
**Website:** heartbeaststudios.com
**YouTube:** youtube.com/uheartbeast
**Twitch:** twitch.tv/uheartbeast
**FaceBook:** facebook.com/heartbeast.studios
**Twitter:** twitter.com/uheartbeast
**Tumblr:** uheartbeast.tumblr.com

## Thanks
Before I show the Kickstarter backer list, I want to say thanks to my wife Charly. She has been a huge support for me in the most frustrating moments. I want to say thank you to my editor Slade. He has been a pleasure to work with and I look forward to working with him more in the future. I want to say thanks to my family and all my friends. I want to say thanks to everybody who emailed me with feedback on this book, especially Chris Sanyk for going above and beyond. And finally, I want to say thanks to you. Thank you for buying my book. Your support means the world to me.

## Stories
If you found this book helpful or inspiring in a very specific way, then email me your story! I will be collecting stories from my readers and YouTube viewers and if your story strikes a chord in my soul, it might be featured in that collection, and sent out with every future copy of my book.

# Top Kickstarter Backers

Here are the top Kickstarter backers. Thank you guys!

- David Almirall - $148.00
- Steven Wise - $100.00
- George Hopper - $82.00
- Jonathon McClung - $80.00 (For USA Shipped Book)

# Kickstarter Backer List

Here is a list of all the other Kickstarter Backers. You guys and gals made this book a reality. Thank you so much!

## $80+ Backers

Bob Morate, Kyle Trehaeven, Floriah Fischer, Chris Ahmad, Robin Playe, Frank Kristiansen, Gera Hmurov, Ingo Liebig, David Till, Robert Parry, Tyler Reddick, Rob Lyndsey, Jono, Markus Lange, Francis Fitzgerald, Lance Tofsrud, Svein Daniel, Solvenus, Jan-Erik Matz, Paul Cook, David Ward, Kevin Scorey, Arthur Uiterwijk, Mathias Nervik, Eleni Merianou, Gustavo Arantes, Tetruashvili, Stelios Potamitis, Chee Lup Wan, Gil Ferrand, DarkCoolEdge, Omar Alterkait, Brodie Helmore, Jose Antunes, Jussi Kukkonen

## $60 Backers

Christopher M. Bell, ReMeX, Lewis Allard, Donovan Anderson, Caleb Anderson, Aaron Freeze, Chinua White, Matthew Jarvis, Chris Sanyk, Demetri Mallous, Quentin Thomas, Matthew Mather, Josh Dresner, James Ryan, Jonathan Wulff, Azuz, Hugo, Zachary Mapes, Trevor Williams, Dallas Bowland, Kenneth Kline, Jonathan Bergeron, Joe Healy, Saadman Rakib, Khan, Stephen Jolly, Uriah Maravilla, Greer, Andrew Jeremy, Goetz, Christopher, Bentley, Kyle Wrigley, Dae in Cho, Scott Goldsmith, EvilLinux, Jeffrey Stockton, Gopal Vithlani, Jean-Denis Haas, Josh Fields, Anna Munoz, Raighne Hogan, Hylyncks, Slade Stolar, Endless Mike, Grant Cable, Natascha Buter, Adrian Lamar, Nick, Daniel Custer, Gregory Lee II, Patrick Polk, James Kaucher, Hamed Al-Riyami

## $30 Backers

Joel Ilett, Alonso, Mikael, Eulogio Enamorado, Pallares, Tom Mason, Matthew Sylvester, Marvan Alkufai, Timothy, Miguel Angel, Garcia Guerra,

Jacob Duffy, Sheldon Sims, Christophe Liaret, Israel RN, Bryan Lumb, Aaron Parsons, Michael Dailly, Diall Delmer, Mats Wallin, Jonathan Johnson, Joe Jerkovic, Jordan Murphy, William Richards, Gamebot School, LLC, Devin Kaufman, Tyrone Swart, Andrew Strauch, Eduardo Augusto, Nicole Imber, Raymond Hegge, Jeff, Jonathan "Ardua", Doyle, Stephen Maden, Carlos, Joe Wilcox, Jon Bursey, Marcio Mattos, Anucha, Wongkarnkah, Gibo, Bob Thulfram, John George, Freed Castillo, RCMADIAX LLC, Faisal Alkubaisi, Baron Beckenham, Bloomer, Javier Martinez, Jeff Watson, Pokemonrey6, John Peterson, Leonid Fadeev, Jaime Chan, Diego Piaggio, Arthur Chan, Carron Ohree, Jonathan, Mcillwaine, Jeremy Lenzo, Jonathan Trafton, Dafydd Francis, Blue Moth Studio, Burnen Thyme, Victor, Andreas Avoukatos, Tyler Sease, Miguel Castro, Marcus Moore, Christian Belding, Chris Sheldon, Jackie, Rodrigo Gomes, Krystof Horacek, Abbenano, Stuart Sulaski, Brian Danforth, David Conover, Lubin Hadalgo, Chris Wahl, Lauri-Martti Kojo, Andrew Rodrigue, David Farina, Melissa Musgrove, Hobbyaescala, Karin Portier, James Clark, Laritza Castaneda, Sven Sowa, Gabriel Quintana, Maik Roseboom, Tasha James, Martin Gebhardt

## $25 Backers

Andrew Gasson, David Jagneaux, Marshall, Tim Hofstee, Hakun, Matthew, Humphries, Tehwave, Alex O'Neill, Jesse Call, Raymond Spiteri, Colonel Fubar, Ildradil, James Rozee, Josh Hash, Federico Colovini, CH Wan, ZpeedTube, Kimmo Savilampi, Philippe Abi Saab, Jonathan Foster, Thryn Henderson, Symbios, William A Burgess, Thrashonkel, Bill Loguidice, Alex Greenwood, Jermain Kanhai, Benjamin Gemmel, Plasma Toy, Studios, Remi D. Finjord, Tommy Wedin, ScyldScefing, Louis Giliberto, Pakoito WooS, Jon Trew, Kyle Frick, Alex Maskill, Matthew Vine, Thomas Herth, PhiRune, Carlos Diaz, Colby Ryan, Maulden, Carlos Martinez, Ben Pledger, Isao Sasaki, Ryan Schuzle, Brian, HyperSloth, Cheryl Howard, Arturo Sanchez, MrNeeNaw, Robert Stockamp, Kong Nyian Sii, Woggos, Toshirolshii, David Brittain, Redstart Industries, Budd Royce, Gabriel Johnson, LazySiege, Cimmarian, Daniel RyJek, Wojcik, John Hoffer, Oscar Bagger, David Batty, Ronald, Alexandre Moisan, Fabiano Martino, Alberto Morales, Gustavo Delgado, Ben Whittaker, Nick Landry, Leong Wai Yin, Hunter Harris, Kevin Pass, c3sk, Marshall Nguyen, Mikael Myntti, Josh, Sam Whillance, Kris King, Dominic, Andreas Sjostrand, Sammywhs, Simone, Claes Wiklund, Spencer, Alexander Hertzler, Malthe, Falkenstjerne, Jorge G, Josh Henry, Steven Guzman, Gunnar Hogberg,

Johann Mayac, Austin Siagian, Andrew, Wooldridge, Felipe Nanni, Rogue Dues, Carolos Navarro, Roman, Fran Orellana, Matthew Hester, Ludvig, Cameron, Simwad, Deepra Smith, Ethan Swords, Paul Broad, Shiki Matsuri, Rishi Ilangovan, Juan Hernandez, RobbyTheChaotic, Janette Leis, Rafal Toczyski, Metatronaut, Antun Kesegic, Romulo Pereira de Araujo, Tom Abbott, Leo Stefaninos, Ralf Zhan, Cosimo Lattanzio, Eka Pramudita Muharram

## $5 Backers
Melissa Anderson Francisco, Slimey Jenkins, Helge Sverre, Greg Mckechnie, Nazariglez, Blue Social Network (Julian), Camijn, Jose Vizcarrondo, Shane Heres, Marilu Aguilar, Brigit Fasolino Vucic, Sean

## $1 Backers
John Sturgill, Leonard Burns IV, Duo, Aaron Zemetres, David Mathias Simacek 2, Tomasz Michal Filip, Kaczmarek

Printed in Great Britain
by Amazon